Elixir Cookbook

Unleash the full power of programming in Elixir with over 60 incredibly effective recipes

Paulo A Pereira

[PACKT] open source *
community experience distilled
PUBLISHING

BIRMINGHAM - MUMBAI

Elixir Cookbook

First published: February 2015

Production reference: 1130215

Published by Packt Publishing Ltd.
Livery Place
35 Livery Street
Birmingham B3 2PB, UK.

ISBN 978-1-78439-751-7

www.packtpub.com

Credits

Author
Paulo A Pereira

Reviewers
Ruhul Amin

Richard Bateman

Craig Beck

Wilson Edgar

Alexei Sholik

Commissioning Editor
Ashwin Nair

Acquisition Editor
Shaon Basu

Content Development Editor
Mohammed Fahad

Technical Editor
Taabish Khan

Copy Editors
Vikrant Phadke

Stuti Srivastava

Project Coordinator
Danuta Jones

Proofreaders
Paul Hindle

Samantha Lyon

Bernadette Watkins

Indexer
Rekha Nair

Production Coordinator
Komal Ramchandani

Cover Work
Komal Ramchandani

About the Author

Paulo A Pereira is a journalist and senior software engineer with a background in Grails and Rails. He fell in love with Elixir and has a passion for exploring new technologies and keeping himself up to date with the industry's developments.

Paulo previously worked as a consultant and lead developer for Mediadigital, implementing Grails and Rails solutions, and he is currently working at Onfido Background Checks, a London-based tech start-up that is proving to be a key player in the background checking industry.

I would like to thank my wife and daughter for their unconditional support. I would also like to thank Wilson for his help and guidance, and José, a true inspiration in his approach to work and life in general.

Finally, I would like to thank all of the reviewers for their valuable comments and the entire Packt Publishing team for their support, especially Fahad, whose kind and steady guidance helped me keep myself on track.

About the Reviewers

Ruhul Amin is the CTO and cofounder of Onfido Background Checks, a company that's revolutionizing the background checking industry. He has a master's degree in engineering from Oxford University. He has been dabbling in Ruby since 2008 and was introduced to Elixir by the author.

Richard Bateman (also sometimes known by his online moniker, "taxilian") has spent the majority of his life developing software. As a child, he was occasionally caught reading development books under the covers with a flashlight, but despite these alarming tendencies, he is married to a wonderful woman and has several wonderful offspring, all of whom did their level best to distract him from helping with this book.

Richard enjoys learning new languages, finding new and creative ways to use old languages, and creatively misusing all languages. He is the original creator and primary maintainer of the open source cross-platform browser plugin framework FireBreath. In his spare time, he works on the popular amateur radio study website HamStudy.org (https://hamstudy.org), and in the rest of his spare time not spent with his family, he works at his day job at GradeCam. If you are a teacher, you need to see what they are doing—check out their work at http://www.gradecam.com.

Richard speaks fluent Russian, rides a motorcycle, makes balloon animals, and is only mildly addicted to software development, no matter what his wife says.

Wilson Edgar is a computer scientist and enthusiast with a passion for learning new programming languages. He loves all that comes with building systems, especially large ones.

When he is not programming, he spends his time with his beautiful family or skateboarding (you're never too old to skateboard).

Alexei Sholik is an enthusiastic developer. He has worked in game development and app development for iOS since 2008, has been contributing to the development of Elixir since 2012, and is currently a member of the Elixir core team. More recently, he got involved in server-side development using Elixir professionally at PSPDFKit.

As a longtime fan of computer science, Alexei enjoys reading an occasional white paper about new advancements and case studies in the field of programming theory and practice while sipping hot tea on a weekend night.

His favorite pastime activities include playing the guitar, learning foreign languages, playing *Riichi,* and imagining what an ideal programming language would look like.

He has reviewed two other books on Elixir and is currently in the process of reviewing *Elixir In Action, Manning Publications.*

www.PacktPub.com

Support files, eBooks, discount offers, and more

For support files and downloads related to your book, please visit www.PacktPub.com.

Did you know that Packt offers eBook versions of every book published, with PDF and ePub files available? You can upgrade to the eBook version at www.PacktPub.com and as a print book customer, you are entitled to a discount on the eBook copy. Get in touch with us at service@packtpub.com for more details.

At www.PacktPub.com, you can also read a collection of free technical articles, sign up for a range of free newsletters and receive exclusive discounts and offers on Packt books and eBooks.

https://www2.packtpub.com/books/subscription/packtlib

Do you need instant solutions to your IT questions? PacktLib is Packt's online digital book library. Here, you can search, access, and read Packt's entire library of books.

Why Subscribe?

- ▶ Fully searchable across every book published by Packt
- ▶ Copy and paste, print, and bookmark content
- ▶ On demand and accessible via a web browser

Free Access for Packt account holders

If you have an account with Packt at www.PacktPub.com, you can use this to access PacktLib today and view 9 entirely free books. Simply use your login credentials for immediate access.

To Rosa and Beatriz

Table of Contents

Preface

More than ever, programmers need tools and languages that enable them to develop applications that take full advantage of all the resources available in a system. A few years ago, programs began to speed up just because CPUs were getting progressively faster. However, the "speed limit" has now been hit, and processors are no longer getting faster.

Instead, we are getting more cores available per chip. Today, the challenge is how to take advantage of all that extra power. Elixir helps us do this!

Elixir is a dynamic, functional programming language created by José Valim. It is compatible with the Erlang virtual machine and ecosystem. It focuses on scalability and fault tolerance. With its concurrency model and its ability to handle distribution seamlessly, it makes the task of implementing resilient and efficient systems easier, even fun!

In this cookbook, you will find recipes covering some of the language tooling and concepts. You will find out that no special powers are needed to write concurrent programs or code that can be executed by other machines. You will find out that all you need is an expressive and powerful language, such as Elixir.

What this book covers

Chapter 1, *Command Line*, introduces Interactive Elixir (IEx), which is a command line tool that allows us to execute and evaluate code. This chapter also introduces Mix, which is an Elixir tool to create and manage projects.

Chapter 2, *Data Types and Structures*, focuses on some concepts of the language: immutability, pattern matching, and lazy evaluation.

Chapter 3, *Strings and Binaries*, shows us how to manipulate strings in Elixir.

Chapter 4, *Modules and Functions*, focuses on the building blocks of Elixir applications, from module directives to pattern matching in function definitions.

Chapter 5, *Processes and Nodes*, shows you that spawning multiple processes to perform asynchronous computations or connecting multiple machines and executing code on any of them is not as hard as it seems. Elixir makes the task easier, and we explore specific examples.

Chapter 6, *OTP – Open Telecom Platform*, talks about OTP, which is a systematization of common programming concepts. It allows us to develop large-scale systems on a solid foundation. In this chapter, we will explore some of its constructs.

Chapter 7, *Cowboy and Phoenix*, is all about the Web! It discusses a range of topics, from serving static files to implementing websockets, or using a fully-featured web framework.

Chapter 8, *Interactions*, interacts with our host operating system and talks about external systems such as Postgresql or Redis. We will also build a Twitter feed parser.

Appendix, *Installation and Further Reading*, covers references for installing Elixir, Redis, and PostgreSQL, as well as for further reading.

What you need for this book

You will need to have Elixir installed as well as Erlang, its only dependency. In this book, we will also be using Postgresql and Redis.

Who this book is for

This book is intended for users with some knowledge of the Elixir language syntax and basic data types/structures. Although this is a cookbook and no sequential reading is required, the book's structure will allow less advanced users who follow it to be gradually exposed to some of Elixir's features and concepts specific to functional programming. To get the most out of this book, you need to have some familiarity with Erlang/Elixir philosophy and concepts.

Sections

In this book, you will find several headings that appear frequently (Getting ready, How to do it, How it works, There's more, and See also).

To give clear instructions on how to complete a recipe, we use these sections as follows:

Getting ready

This section tells you what to expect in the recipe, and describes how to set up any software or any preliminary settings required for the recipe.

How to do it...

This section contains the steps required to follow the recipe.

How it works...

This section usually consists of a detailed explanation of what happened in the previous section.

There's more...

This section consists of additional information about the recipe in order to make the reader more knowledgeable about the recipe.

See also

This section provides helpful links to other useful information for the recipe.

Conventions

In this book, you will find a number of text styles that distinguish between different kinds of information. Here are some examples of these styles and an explanation of their meaning.

Code words in text, database table names, folder names, filenames, file extensions, pathnames, dummy URLs, user input, and Twitter handles are shown as follows: "The Elixir standard library has a `List` module defined."

A block of code is set as follows:

```
code\greeter.ex
defmodule Greeter do
def greet(name \\ "you") do
"Hello #{name} !"
end
end
```

When we wish to draw your attention to a particular part of a code block, the relevant lines or items are set in bold:

```
supervised_app/mix.exs
def application do
  [applications: [:logger],
  mod: {SupervisedApp, []}]
end
```

Any command-line input or output is written as follows:

```
> mix help
```

New terms and **important words** are shown in bold. Words that you see on the screen, for example, in menus or dialog boxes, appear in the text like this: "Select the **Load Charts** tab to see graphical representation of memory usage, IO, and scheduler utilization over time."

 Warnings or important notes appear in a box like this.

 Tips and tricks appear like this.

Reader feedback

Feedback from our readers is always welcome. Let us know what you think about this book—what you liked or disliked. Reader feedback is important for us as it helps us develop titles that you will really get the most out of.

To send us general feedback, simply e-mail feedback@packtpub.com, and mention the book's title in the subject of your message.

If there is a topic that you have expertise in and you are interested in either writing or contributing to a book, see our author guide at www.packtpub.com/authors.

Customer support

Now that you are the proud owner of a Packt book, we have a number of things to help you to get the most from your purchase.

Downloading the example code

You can download the example code files from your account at http://www.packtpub.com for all the Packt Publishing books you have purchased. If you purchased this book elsewhere, you can visit http://www.packtpub.com/support and register to have the files e-mailed directly to you.

Errata

Although we have taken every care to ensure the accuracy of our content, mistakes do happen. If you find a mistake in one of our books—maybe a mistake in the text or the code—we would be grateful if you could report this to us. By doing so, you can save other readers from frustration and help us improve subsequent versions of this book. If you find any errata, please report them by visiting `http://www.packtpub.com/submit-errata`, selecting your book, clicking on the **Errata Submission Form** link, and entering the details of your errata. Once your errata are verified, your submission will be accepted and the errata will be uploaded to our website or added to any list of existing errata under the Errata section of that title.

To view the previously submitted errata, go to `https://www.packtpub.com/books/content/support` and enter the name of the book in the search field. The required information will appear under the **Errata** section.

Piracy

Piracy of copyrighted material on the Internet is an ongoing problem across all media. At Packt, we take the protection of our copyright and licenses very seriously. If you come across any illegal copies of our works in any form on the Internet, please provide us with the location address or website name immediately so that we can pursue a remedy.

Please contact us at `copyright@packtpub.com` with a link to the suspected pirated material.

We appreciate your help in protecting our authors and our ability to bring you valuable content.

Questions

If you have a problem with any aspect of this book, you can contact us at `questions@packtpub.com`, and we will do our best to address the problem.

1
Command Line

This chapter will cover the following recipes:

- ▶ Interactive Elixir (IEx):
    - ❑ Using the terminal to prototype and test ideas
    - ❑ Loading and compiling modules
    - ❑ Getting help and accessing documentation within IEx
    - ❑ Using Erlang from Elixir
    - ❑ Inspecting your system in IEx
    - ❑ Inspecting your system with Observer

- ▶ Mix:
    - ❑ Creating a simple application
    - ❑ Managing dependencies
    - ❑ Generating a supervised application
    - ❑ Generating umbrella applications
    - ❑ Managing application configuration
    - ❑ Creating custom Mix tasks

Introduction

The command line is the preferred way to create and interact with Elixir applications, inspect running systems, and prototype ideas.

Interactive Elixir (**IEx**) allows immediate evaluation of any expression, and it is also possible to define modules directly without saving them previously on a file. Similar tools exist in other programming languages; Ruby's IRB or Clojure's REPL are some examples.

Mix is a build tool that provides several tasks to create, compile, and test projects, and handle dependencies. It is also possible to define custom tasks with Mix. In the *Creating custom Mix tasks* recipe, we will create a task to display the memory usage. It is common for some applications to define their own tasks. Phoenix framework (which will be covered in *Chapter 7*, *Cowboy and Phoenix*) is just one example of this.

Using the terminal to prototype and test ideas

The Elixir default installation provides an **REPL** (short for **read-eval-print-loop**) named IEx. IEx is a programming environment that takes user expressions, evaluates them, and returns the result to the user. This allows the user to test code and even create entire modules, without having to compile a source file.

To start prototyping or testing some ideas, all we need to do is use IEx via our command line.

Getting ready

To get started, we need to have Elixir installed. Instructions on how to install Elixir can be found at `http://elixir-lang.org/install.html`. This page covers installation on OSX, Unix and Unix-like systems, and Windows. It also gives some instructions on how to install Erlang, which is the only prerequisite to run Elixir.

How to do it...

To prototype and test the ideas using IEx, follow these steps:

1. Start IEx by typing `iex` in your command line.
2. Type some expressions and have them evaluated:

```
iex(1)> a = 2 + 2
4
iex(2)> b = a * a
16
iex(3)> a + b
```

```
20

iex(4)>
```

3. Define an anonymous function to add two numbers:

    ```
    iex(5)> sum = fn(a, b) -> a + b end
    Function<12.90072148/2 in :erl_eval.expr/5>
    ```

4. Invoke the function to add two numbers:

    ```
    iex(6)> sum.(1,2)
    3
    ```

5. Quit from IEx by pressing _Ctrl + C_ twice.

How it works...

IEx evaluates expressions as they are typed, allowing us to get instant feedback. This allows and encourages experimenting ideas without the overhead of editing a source file and compiling it in order to see any changes made.

> In this recipe, we used the = operator. Unlike other languages, = is not an assignment operator but a pattern matching operator. We will get into more detail on pattern matching in the _Using pattern matching_ and _Pattern matching an HTTPoison response_ recipes in _Chapter 2, Data Types and Structures_.
>
> In step 3, we used a dot (.) in the sum function right before the arguments, like this: sum.(1,2). The dot is used to call the anonymous function.

There's more...

It is possible to define modules inside an IEx session.

Loading and compiling modules

It is possible to load code from source files into an IEx session. Multiple modules may be loaded and used, allowing us to incorporate existing code into our prototyping or idea testing session.

Getting ready

In this recipe, we will be importing two files that define the `Greeter` and `Echoer` modules into our IEx session.

In the following lines, we will list the contents of these modules:

```
code\greeter.ex
defmodule Greeter do

  def greet(name \\ "you") do
    "Hello #{name} !"
  end

end

code/echoer.ex
defmodule Echoer do

  def echo(msg) do
    IO.puts "#{msg} ... #{msg} ...... #{msg}"
  end

end
```

Downloading the example code

You can download the example code files from your account at `http://www.packtpub.com` for all the Packt Publishing books you have purchased. If you purchased this book elsewhere, you can visit `http://www.packtpub.com/support` and register to have the files e-mailed directly to you.

How to do it...

We will follow these steps to load and compile the modules:

1. Start IEx:

   iex

2. Load the `Greeter` module defined in `greeter.ex`:

   iex(1)> c("greeter.ex")

   [Greeter]

3. Load the `Echoer` module defined in `echoer.ex`:

   ```
   iex(2)> c("echoer.ex")
   [Echoer]
   ```

4. Use the `greet` function defined in the `Greeter` module:

   ```
   iex(3)> Greeter.greet("Me")
   "Hello Me !"
   ```

5. Use the `echo` function defined in the `Echoer` module:

   ```
   iex(4)> Echoer.echo("hello")
   hello ... hello ...... hello
   :ok
   ```

6. Combine the functions defined in both modules:

   ```
   iex(7)> Greeter.greet("Me") |> Echoer.echo
   Hello Me ! ... Hello Me ! ...... Hello Me !
   :ok
   ```

 Some functions may have default values. They are denoted by the use of \\. In the `Greeter` module, the `greet` function is defined as `def greet(name \\ "you")`, which means that if we omit the argument passed to the function, it will default to you.

How it works...

When `c("file_name.ex")` is invoked from IEx, the file is loaded and compiled (a corresponding file with the `.beam` extension will be created).

The module (or modules) defined on each imported file become available. It is possible to invoke functions on these modules using the `ModuleName.function_name(args)` syntax.

If a `module_name.beam` file exists for a given module, then every time you import that module into an IEx session, you will see the following warning:

```
module_name.ex:1: warning: redefining module ModuleName
```

The warning means that a new compiled `.beam` file is being created, potentially redefining the module. If no changes were made to the source code, the code will be the same, although the warning is still issued.

In step 6, the pipe operator (`|>`) is used to simplify the code. This operator means that the output of the left operation will be fed as the first argument to the right operation.

This is equivalent to writing the following:

```
Echoer.echo(Greeter.greet("Me"))
```

There's more...

In steps 2 and 3, the `greeter.ex` and `echoer.ex` files are imported without indicating the path because they are under the same directory from where the IEx session was started.

It is possible to use relative or full paths when loading files:

- We can use relative paths like this:

    ```
    iex(1)> c("../greeter.ex")
    ```

- We can use full paths like this:

    ```
    iex(2)> c("/home/user/echoer.ex")
    ```

 Note that the `c` IEx function accepts a string as an argument.

Getting help and accessing documentation within IEx

Documentation is a first-class citizen in the Elixir ecosystem, so it comes as no surprise that IEx provides convenient ways to access documentation and get help without the need to leave an IEx session.

This recipe exemplifies the use of the defined help functions.

How to do it...

We will follow these steps to get help and access documentation in an IEx session:

1. Enter `h` inside a running IEx session to see the help options related to the use of IEx helpers, as shown in this screenshot:

```
iex(2)> h
```

```
                                IEx.Helpers

Welcome to Interactive Elixir. You are currently seeing the documentation for
the module IEx.Helpers which provides many helpers to make Elixir's shell more
joyful to work with.

This message was triggered by invoking the helper h(), usually referred to as
h/0 (since it expects 0 arguments).

There are many other helpers available:

  · c/2         - compiles a file at the given path
  · cd/1        - changes the current directory
  · clear/0     - clears the screen
  · flush/0     - flushes all messages sent to the shell
  · h/0         - prints this help message
  · h/1         - prints help for the given module, function or macro
  · l/1         - loads the given module's beam code and purges the current
  version
  · ls/0        - lists the contents of the current directory
  · ls/1        - lists the contents of the specified directory
  · pwd/0       - prints the current working directory
  · r/1         - recompiles and reloads the given module's source file
  · respawn/0 - respawns the current shell
  · s/1         - prints spec information
  · t/1         - prints type information
  · v/0         - prints the history of commands evaluated in the session
  · v/1         - retrieves the nth value from the history
  · import_file/1
    |           - evaluates the given file in the shell's context


Help for functions in this module can be consulted directly from the command
line, as an example, try:

| h(c/2)

You can also retrieve the documentation for any module or function. Try these:

| h(Enum)
| h(Enum.reverse/1)

To learn more about IEx as a whole, just type h(IEx).

iex(3)> _
```

2. If we wish, for instance, to get information regarding the `c/2` function, we type `h(c/2)`, as shown in the following screenshot:

```
iex(2)> h(c/2)

                        def c(files, path \\ ".")

Expects a list of files to compile and a path to write their object code to. It
returns the name of the compiled modules.

When compiling one file, there is no need to wrap it in a list.

Examples

| c ["foo.ex", "bar.ex"], "ebin"
| #=> [Foo,Bar]
|
| c "baz.ex"
| #=> [Baz]

iex(3)>
```

3. Accessing a module documentation is done by invoking `h(ModuleName)`. In the next screenshot, we access documentation related to `Enum`:

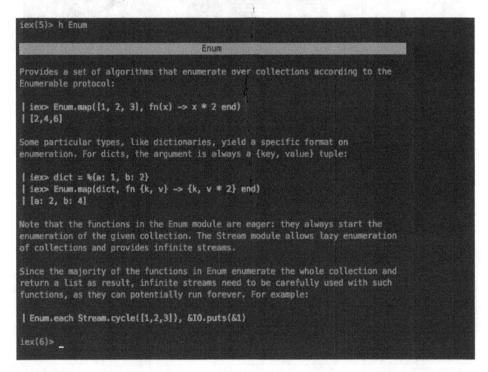

```
iex(5)> h Enum

                                  Enum

Provides a set of algorithms that enumerate over collections according to the
Enumerable protocol:

| iex> Enum.map([1, 2, 3], fn(x) -> x * 2 end)
| [2,4,6]

Some particular types, like dictionaries, yield a specific format on
enumeration. For dicts, the argument is always a {key, value} tuple:

| iex> dict = %{a: 1, b: 2}
| iex> Enum.map(dict, fn {k, v} -> {k, v * 2} end)
| [a: 2, b: 4]

Note that the functions in the Enum module are eager: they always start the
enumeration of the given collection. The Stream module allows lazy enumeration
of collections and provides infinite streams.

Since the majority of the functions in Enum enumerate the whole collection and
return a list as result, infinite streams need to be carefully used with such
functions, as they can potentially run forever. For example:

| Enum.each Stream.cycle([1,2,3]), &IO.puts(&1)

iex(6)>
```

4. Getting information about a specific function inside a module is also possible by invoking h(ModuleName.function_name). The following screenshot shows the documentation for Enum.map:

```
iex(7)> h Enum.map

                        def map(collection, fun)

Returns a new collection, where each item is the result of invoking fun on each
corresponding item of collection.

For dicts, the function expects a key-value tuple.

Examples

 | iex> Enum.map([1, 2, 3], fn(x) -> x * 2 end)
 | [2, 4, 6]
 |
 | iex> Enum.map([a: 1, b: 2], fn({k, v}) -> {k, -v} end)
 | [a: -1, b: -2]

iex(8)> _
```

How it works...

When we define modules, it is possible to use the @moduledoc and @doc annotations to define documentation related to the whole module or to a specific function in that module.

IEx parses the documentation defined with these annotations and makes it available in a convenient way so that there's no need to leave the session when help or some more information is needed.

IEx itself has several helper functions defined (refer to the first screenshot of this recipe), and among them, we find h/0 and h/1.

 It is common to refer to functions by their name followed by / and a number indicating the number of arguments that function takes. Therefore, h/0 is a function named h that takes 0 arguments, and h/1 is the same h function but with 1 argument.

There's more...

There are several defined functions that allow accessing information on function specifications and types (if defined). To learn more, you can use s/1 and t/1.

As an example, to get information on the types defined for the Enum module, we would use t(Enum), and to get information on the specifications, we would use s(Enum).

Using Erlang from Elixir

Elixir code runs in the Erlang VM. The ability to invoke Erlang code from within Elixir allows the use of resources from the entire Erlang ecosystem, and since Elixir code is compiled to the same byte code as Erlang code, there is no performance penalty.

It is also possible to include in an Elixir application the Erlang code that is already compiled.

If you take a closer look, the files we compile in IEx sessions have the .beam extension, and that's exactly the same format Erlang's compiled code gets transformed into.

Getting ready

To use Erlang code in Elixir, we start a new IEx session.

How to do it...

These are some examples of how to invoke Erlang code from Elixir:

1. Erlang's `Application` module defines a function named `which_applications`. This function returns a list of applications being executed in an Erlang VM. This is the way to use this function from Elixir:

   ```
   iex(1)> :application.which_applications
   ```

    The Erlang code would be `application:which_applications()`.

2. To get information on any Erlang module, there is a function named `module_info`. To know more about the `erlang` module, we enter this:

   ```
   iex(2)> :erlang.module_info
   ```

    The Erlang code would be `erlang:module_info()`.

How it works...

In Elixir, Erlang modules are represented as atoms. Functions in these modules are invoked in the same way as any Elixir function.

In Elixir, the atom type is used as an identifier for a given value. In Ruby, the equivalent of the atom is known as the **symbol**.

There's more...

Existing Erlang libraries can be included in Elixir applications, widening the available options. It is also possible to choose an Erlang implementation of a module over Elixir's.

The Elixir standard library has a `List` module defined. The Erlang counterpart is `lists`.

If we wish to get the last element of a list, we could use both modules:

- We can use Elixir's `List` module like this:

```
List.last([1,2,3])
```

- We can use Erlang's `lists` module in this manner:

```
:lists.last([1,2,3])
```

 The Erlang code for this operation is `lists:last([1,2,3])`.

Inspecting your system in IEx

Sometimes, we need to take a look at what is going on in a running VM. It is useful to see which applications are open and any information about memory usage.

We will use some Erlang modules to inspect a VM instance.

Getting ready

Start a new IEx session.

How to do it...

We will follow these steps to get information on our running system:

1. To get the currently running applications, type this:

```
iex(1)> :application.which_applications
[
  {:logger, 'logger', '0.15.1'},
```

```
    {:iex, 'iex', '0.15.1'},
    {:elixir, 'elixir', '0.15.1'},
    {:syntax_tools, 'Syntax tools', '1.6.15'},
    {:compiler, 'ERTS  CXC 138 10', '5.0.1'},
    {:crypto, 'CRYPTO', '3.4'},
    {:stdlib, 'ERTS  CXC 138 10', '2.1'},
    {:kernel, 'ERTS  CXC 138 10', '3.0.1'}
]
```

The list that is returned contains three-element tuples. The first element is an atom identifying the application, the second element is the application description, and the third is the application version.

2. We get information on the memory usage by running the following commands:

```
iex(2)> :erlang.memory
[total: 15474240, processes: 4958016, processes_used: 4957056,
system: 10516224,
 atom: 256313, atom_used: 234423, binary: 15352, code: 6071692,
ets: 399560]
```

3. It is also possible to get memory usage for atoms, ets tables, binaries, and so on:

```
iex(3)> :erlang.memory(:atom)
256313
```

How it works...

As we saw in the previous recipe, *Using Erlang from Elixir*, it is possible to seamlessly call Erlang code from Elixir. Even though there is no specific Elixir code to perform these inspections, it is easy to get these abilities via Erlang libraries.

See also

▶ When a GUI environment is available, there's a tool called Observer that helps to get information on an Erlang VM. Take a look at the next recipe, *Inspecting your system with Observer*.

Inspecting your system with Observer

The command line isn't the only way to get information on an Erlang VM. There is a GUI tool named Observer that allows access to information in a more convenient way.

If a GUI-enabled system is available, Observer allows us to open multiple windows with information on the whole system's statistics or even an individual process of that running system.

Getting ready

Start an IEx session.

How to do it...

To use the Observer GUI application, we will follow these steps:

1. Start the Observer application:

   ```
   iex(1)> :observer.start
   :ok
   ```

2. A new window with a tabbed interface will open, and the first information displayed shows CPU information, memory usage, system information, and statistics, as shown in the following screenshot:

3. Select the **Load Charts** tab to see graphical representation of memory usage, IO, and scheduler utilization over time, as shown here:

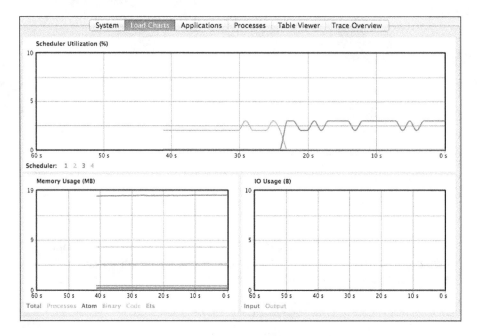

4. Under the **Applications** tab, by selecting the **kernel** application, it is possible to see a representation of an application process's hierarchy, as shown in this screenshot:

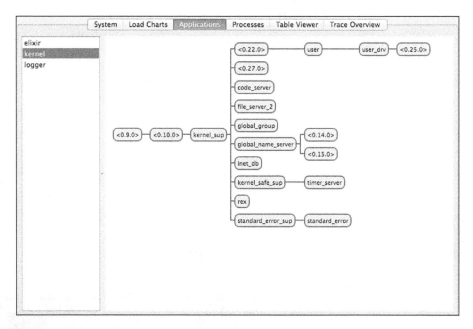

5. Double-click on any of the nodes, for example, `code_server`. A new window will be opened with information for the specific process, as shown in the following screenshot:

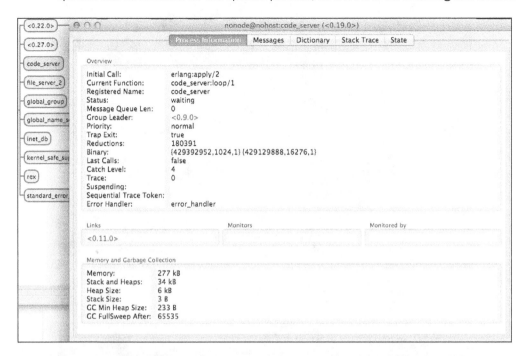

Creating a simple application

In this recipe, we will be using Mix to create a new application.

How to do it...

To create a new Elixir application, follow these steps:

1. In a command-line session, enter `mix help` to see a list of available tasks:

```
> mix help
```

Here is what the screen will look like:

```
> mix help
mix                     # Run the default task (current: mix run)
mix archive             # List all archives
mix archive.build       # Archive this project into a .ez file
mix archive.install     # Install an archive locally
mix archive.uninstall   # Uninstall archives
mix clean               # Delete generated application files
mix cmd                 # Executes the given command
mix compile             # Compile source files
mix compile.protocols   # Consolidates all protocols in all paths
mix deps                # List dependencies and their status
mix deps.clean          # Remove the given dependencies' files
mix deps.compile        # Compile dependencies
mix deps.get            # Get all out of date dependencies
mix deps.unlock         # Unlock the given dependencies
mix deps.update         # Update the given dependencies
mix dialyzer            # Runs dialyzer with default or project-defined flags.
mix dialyzer.plt        # Builds PLT with default erlang applications included.
mix do                  # Executes the tasks separated by comma
mix escript.build       # Builds an escript for the project
mix help                # Print help information for tasks
mix hex.config          # Read or update hex config
mix hex.info            # Print hex information
mix hex.key             # Hex API key tasks
mix hex.owner           # Hex package ownership tasks
mix hex.publish         # Publish a new package version
mix hex.search          # Search for package names
mix hex.user            # Hex user tasks
mix loadconfig          # Loads and persists the given configuration
mix local               # List local tasks
mix local.hex           # Install hex locally
mix local.rebar         # Install rebar locally
mix new                 # Create a new Elixir project
mix run                 # Run the given file or expression
mix test                # Run a project's tests
iex -S mix              # Start IEx and run the default task
```

2. To generate a new application, type `mix new simple_app`:

> **mix new simple_app**

What happens next is shown in the following screenshot:

```
> mix new simple_app
* creating README.md
* creating .gitignore
* creating mix.exs
* creating config
* creating config/config.exs
* creating lib
* creating lib/simple_app.ex
* creating test
* creating test/test_helper.exs
* creating test/simple_app_test.exs

Your mix project was created successfully.
You can use mix to compile it, test it, and more:

    cd simple_app
    mix test

Run `mix help` for more commands.
```

3. Inside the `simple_app` directory, the generated application is ready to be started. Run `iex -S mix` to start the application and verify that everything is working:

```
> iex -S mix
Erlang/OTP 17 [erts-6.1] [source] [64-bit] [smp:4:4] [async-threads:10] [hipe] [kernel-poll:false] [dtrace]
Interactive Elixir (0.15.1) - press Ctrl+C to exit (type h() ENTER for help)
iex(1)>
```

4. Nothing happened. So is it working? The absence of messages in the IEx session is a good thing. This generated application behaves more like a library; there's no `main` function like in Java or C. To be sure that the application is responding, edit the `lib/simple_app.ex` file by inserting the following code:

```
defmodule SimpleApp do
  def greet do
    IO.puts "Hello from Simple App!"
  end
end
```

5. Restart the application by pressing *Ctrl + C* twice and entering `iex -S mix` again.

6. In the IEx session, enter `SimpleApp.greet`.

7. You will see the following output from the application:

```
iex(1)> SimpleApp.greet
Hello from Simple App!
:ok
iex(2)>
```

The Elixir application is ready to be used either on your local machine or, if a node is started, it could even be used from another machine.

How it works...

The Elixir installation provides a command-line tool called Mix. Mix is a build tool. With this tool, it is possible to invoke several tasks to create applications, manage their dependencies, run them, and more.

Mix even allows the creation of custom tasks.

See also

▸ To generate an OTP application with a supervisor, see the *Generating a supervised application* recipe.

Managing dependencies

One of the advantages of OTP (more information on OTP may be found in *Chapter 6, OTP – Open Telecom Platform*) is modularity, and it is very common to have several applications running as dependencies of one application. An application is a way to achieve modularity; in this context, we call an application something that is known in other programming languages as a library. In this recipe, we will integrate an HTTP client with a new application. We will be using the Hex package manager (http://hex.pm).

Getting ready

1. Generate a new application with `mix new manage_deps`:

   ```
   > mix new manage_deps
   ```

   The output is shown in the following screenshot:

   ```
   > mix new manage_deps
   * creating README.md
   * creating .gitignore
   * creating mix.exs
   * creating config
   * creating config/config.exs
   * creating lib
   * creating lib/manage_deps.ex
   * creating test
   * creating test/test_helper.exs
   * creating test/manage_deps_test.exs

   Your mix project was created successfully.
   You can use mix to compile it, test it, and more:

       cd manage_deps
       mix test

   Run `mix help` for more commands.
   ```

2. Visit `https://hex.pm/packages?search=http`.
3. We will choose HTTPoison (`https://hex.pm/packages/httpoison`).

How to do it...

To add a dependency to our application, we will follow these steps:

1. Inside the `manage_deps` application, open `mix.exs` and edit the file to include HTTPoison as a dependency:

    ```
    defp deps do
        [{:httpoison, "~> 0.4"}]
    end
    ```

2. HTTPoison must be started with our system. Add this to the started applications list by including it inside the `application` function:

    ```
    def application do
        [applications: [:logger, :httpoison]]
    end
    ```

3. Save `mix.exs` and run `mix deps.get` to fetch the declared dependencies, as shown in this screenshot:

    ```
    > mix deps.get
    * Getting httpoison (package)
    Checking package (http://s3.hex.pm/tarballs/httpoison-0.4.2.tar)
    Using locally cached package
    Unpacked package tarball (/Users/paulopereira/.hex/packages/httpoison-0.4.2.tar)
    * Getting hackney (package)
    Checking package (http://s3.hex.pm/tarballs/hackney-0.13.1.tar)
    Using locally cached package
    Unpacked package tarball (/Users/paulopereira/.hex/packages/hackney-0.13.1.tar)
    * Getting idna (package)
    Checking package (http://s3.hex.pm/tarballs/idna-1.0.1.tar)
    Using locally cached package
    Unpacked package tarball (/Users/paulopereira/.hex/packages/idna-1.0.1.tar)
    ```

4. Compile the dependencies by executing `mix deps.compile`, as shown in the following screenshot:

```
> mix deps.compile
==> idna (compile)
Compiled src/punycode.erl
Compiled src/idna_unicode.erl
Compiled src/idna.erl
Compiled src/idna_ucs.erl
Compiled src/idna_unicode_data.erl
==> hackney (compile)
Compiled src/hackney_connect/hackney_pool_handler.erl
Compiled src/hackney_lib/hackney_multipart.erl
Compiled src/hackney_lib/hackney_url.erl
Compiled src/hackney_lib/hackney_http.erl
Compiled src/hackney_lib/hackney_headers.erl
Compiled src/hackney_lib/hackney_cookie.erl
Compiled src/hackney_lib/hackney_date.erl
Compiled src/hackney_connect/hackney_tcp_transport.erl
Compiled src/hackney_connect/hackney_ssl_transport.erl
Compiled src/hackney_lib/hackney_bstr.erl
Compiled src/hackney_connect/hackney_socks5.erl
Compiled src/hackney_connect/hackney_http_connect.erl
Compiled src/hackney_connect/hackney_pool.erl
Compiled src/hackney_client/hackney_util.erl
Compiled src/hackney_connect/hackney_connect.erl
Compiled src/hackney_client/hackney_stream.erl
Compiled src/hackney_client/hackney_response.erl
Compiled src/hackney_client/hackney_manager.erl
Compiled src/hackney_client/hackney_idna.erl
Compiled src/hackney_client/hackney_request.erl
Compiled src/hackney_app/hackney_sup.erl
Compiled src/hackney_app/hackney_deps.erl
Compiled src/hackney_app/hackney_app.erl
Compiled src/hackney_client/hackney.erl
Compiled src/hackney_lib/hackney_mimetypes.erl
==> httpoison
Compiled lib/httpoison/base.ex
Compiled lib/httpoison.ex
Generated httpoison.app
```

 Sometimes, some of the dependencies are Erlang projects, so you may get a prompt asking you to install rebar (rebar is a tool similar to Mix used in Erlang projects). Once you accept to download it, it will be available in your system and you won't have to worry about it anymore.

5. Start your application with `iex -S mix`.

6. Inside the IEx session, check whether HTTPoison is running:

```
iex(1)> :application.which_applications
[{:manage_deps, 'manage_deps', '0.0.1'},
  {:httpoison, ' Yet Another HTTP client for Elixir powered by
hackney\n',
   '0.4.2'}, {:hackney, 'simple HTTP client', '0.13.1'}(…)]
```

7. Get Google's main page using HTTPoison:

```
iex(5)> HTTPoison.get("http://www.google.com")
%HTTPoison.Response{body: "<HTML><HEAD><meta http-equiv=\"content-
type\" content=\"text/html;charset=utf-8\">\n<TITLE>302 Moved</
TITLE></HEAD><BODY>\n<H1>302 Moved</H1>\nThe document has moved\
n<A HREF=\"http://www.google.pt/?gfe_rd=cr&amp;ei=WFAOVLvQFJSs8wfe
hYJg\">here</A>.\r\n</BODY></HTML>\r\n",
  headers: %{"Alternate-Protocol" => "80:quic", "Cache-Control" =>
"private",
    "Content-Length" => "256", "Content-Type" => "text/html;
      charset=UTF-8",
    "Date" => "Tue, 09 Sep 2014 00:56:56 GMT",
    "Location" => "http://www.google.pt/?gfe_rd=cr&
      ei=WFAOVLvQFJSs8wfehYJg",
    "Server" => "GFE/2.0"}, status_code: 302}
```

How it works...

Dependencies are preferably added using hex.pm (`https://hex.pm/`).

> If an application doesn't yet exist in Hex, it is also possible to use a GitHub repository as a source.
>
> To fetch a dependency from GitHub, instead of declaring the dependency with the `{:httpoison, "~> 0.4"}` format, the following format is used:
>
> `{:httpoison, github: " edgurgel/httpoison "}`
>
> The local filesystem may also be configured as a source for dependencies, as follows:
>
> `{:httpotion, path: "path/to/httpotion"}`

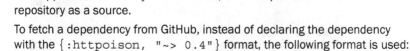

Once the dependencies are declared inside the `mix.exs` file, there are Mix tasks to get, compile, and clean them. The dependencies are then fetched, and if these dependencies have more dependencies on themselves, Mix is smart enough to fetch them.

When compiling dependencies, Mix is also capable of figuring out whether any dependent application has its own dependencies and whether they need to be compiled.

Starting IEx with the −s Mix loads the Mix environment inside IEx, and the application becomes accessible.

As shown in the *Inspecting your system* recipe, it is possible to get a list of running applications and check whether our dependency (and its own dependencies) are running. In the particular case of HTTPoison, automatic start is ensured by adding the atom representing the application name to the list under `applications([applications: [:logger, :httpoison]])`.

See also

▶   The documentation on Hex usage available at `https://hex.pm/docs/usage`.

▶   The Elixir documentation on Mix tasks is available at `http://elixir-lang.org/docs/stable/mix/`.

Generating a supervised application

An application may be generated with a supervision tree to monitor processes. The supervision tree must be started and stopped with the application, and to do so, an application module callback must also be implemented. Mix provides a simple way to generate this type of application.

How to do it...

To generate an application with a supervision tree and an application module callback, we run `mix new supervised_app --sup` in the command line. This is shown in the following screenshot:

```
> mix new supervised_app --sup
* creating README.md
* creating .gitignore
* creating mix.exs
* creating config
* creating config/config.exs
* creating lib
* creating lib/supervised_app.ex
* creating test
* creating test/test_helper.exs
* creating test/supervised_app_test.exs

Your mix project was created successfully.
You can use mix to compile it, test it, and more:

    cd supervised_app
    mix test

Run `mix help` for more commands.
```

How it works...

When `mix new task` is invoked with the `--sup` option, although the generated application appears to be identical to the application created in the *Creating a simple application* recipe, a few things change, which are as follows:

```
supervised_app/mix.exs
def application do
  [applications: [:logger],
  mod: {SupervisedApp, []}]
end
```

An application module callback is added like this:

```
supervised_app/lib/supervised_app.ex
defmodule SupervisedApp do
  use Application
  def start(_type, _args) do
    import Supervisor.Spec, warn: false
    children = [
      # Define workers and child supervisors to be supervised
      # worker(SupervisedApp.Worker, [arg1, arg2, arg3])
    ]
    opts = [strategy: :one_for_one, name:
      SupervisedApp.Supervisor]
    Supervisor.start_link(children, opts)
  end
end
```

The `Application` module behavior is declared, and a `start` function must be defined to comply with this behavior. Inside the `start` function, a list of children (usually worker processes) is declared, and so are the supervision options (`opts`). The supervisor is then started, passing the list of processes to be supervised and the options.

See also

- The documentation for the `Application` module can be accessed at `http://elixir-lang.org/docs/stable/elixir/Application.html`.
- Information on the `Supervisor` module is available at `http://elixir-lang.org/docs/stable/elixir/Supervisor.html`.

Generating umbrella applications

The "Erlang way" is to name each self-contained unit of code as an app. Sometimes, an app may be what is referred to as a library in other languages. This is a great way to achieve code reusability and modularity, but sometimes, it is convenient to treat all the apps in a project as a single entity, committing them as a whole to version control, to allow running tests, and so on. Think of an umbrella application as a container used to hold one or more applications and to make them behave as a single application.

This recipe shows how to create umbrella applications with Mix.

How to do it...

1. Generate an umbrella application to contain other applications:

   ```
   mix new --umbrella container
   ```

   What happens next is shown in the following screenshot:

   ```
   > mix new —umbrella container
   * creating .gitignore
   * creating README.md
   * creating mix.exs
   * creating apps
   * creating config
   * creating config/config.exs

   Your umbrella project was created successfully.
   Inside your project, you will find an apps/ directory
   where you can create and host many apps:

       cd container
       cd apps
       mix new my_app

   Commands like `mix compile` and `mix test` when executed
   in the umbrella project root will automatically run
   for each application in the apps/ directory.
   ```

2. Generate `application_one` and `application_two` inside the `container/apps` directory:

   ```
   > cd container/apps
   ```

   ```
   > mix new application_one
   ```

   ```
   > mix new application_two
   ```

3. Modify the tests in the applications as follows:

    ❑ Change the test in `container/apps/application_one/application_one_test.exs` like this:

    ```
    test "the truth on application one" do
      IO.puts "Running Application One tests"
      assert 1 + 1 == 2
    end
    ```

    ❑ Change the test in `container/apps/application_two/application_two_test.exs` as shown here:

    ```
    test "the truth on application two" do
      IO.puts "Running Application Two tests"
      assert 2 - 1 == 1
    end
    ```

4. Run the tests in all applications (inside the container directory):

    ```
    > mix test
    ```

    The result of these tests is shown here:

    ```
    > mix test
    ==> application_two
    Running Application Two tests
    .

    Finished in 0.04 seconds (0.04s on load, 0.00s on tests)
    1 tests, 0 failures

    Randomized with seed 41707
    ==> application_one
    Running Application One tests
    .

    Finished in 0.00 seconds
    1 tests, 0 failures
    ```

5. Now run the tests individually. Firstly, run them for `application_one` as follows:

    ```
    > cd apps/application_one
    ```

    ```
    > mix test
    ```

The outcome of these tests is shown in the following screenshot:

```
> mix test
Running Application One tests

.

Finished in 0.04 seconds (0.04s on load, 0.00s on tests)
1 tests, 0 failures
```

For `application_two`, run them like this:

```
> cd ../application_two
> mix test
```

The result of these tests is shown in this screenshot:

```
> mix test
Running Application Two tests

.

Finished in 0.04 seconds (0.04s on load, 0.00s on tests)
1 tests, 0 failures
```

How it works...

By generating this structure of the application with subprojects under the `apps` directory, Elixir makes dependency management, compilation, and testing easier. It is possible to perform these tasks at the umbrella application level, affecting all the subprojects, or at each subproject level, allowing a high level of granularity.

See also

▶ The Elixir *Getting Started* guide on dependencies and umbrella projects is available at `http://elixir-lang.org/getting_started/mix_otp/7.html`. It says the following:

> *Remember that the runtime and the Elixir ecosystem already provide the concept of applications. As such, we expect you to frequently break your code into applications that can be organized logically, even within a single project. However, if you push every application as a separate project to a Git repository, your projects can become very hard to maintain, because now you will have to spend a lot of time managing those Git repositories rather than writing your code.*

For this reason, Mix supports "umbrella projects." Umbrella projects allow you to create one project that hosts many applications and push all of them to a single Git repository. That is exactly the style we are going to explore in the next sections.

Managing application configuration

Mix tasks run in a specific environment. The predefined environments are production, development, and test (**prod**, **dev**, and **test**). The default environment is dev. In this recipe, we will configure an application with different values for each environment. Invoking the same function will result in a different output based on the configuration.

How to do it...

To manage an application configuration, we follow these steps:

1. Create a new application:

    ```
    > mix new config_example
    ```

2. Go to the generated application directory and open `config/config.exs`.

3. Replace all of the file's content with the following code:

    ```
    use Mix.Config

    config :config_example,
      message_one: "This is a shared message!"

    import_config "#{Mix.env}.exs"
    ```

4. Create three more files under the `config` directory with the following code:

    ❑ In `config/dev.exs`, add the following:

    ```
    use Mix.Config

    config :config_example,
      message_two: "I'm a development environment message!"
    ```

    ❑ In `config/prod.exs`, add this code:

    ```
    use Mix.Config

    config :config_example,
      message_two: "I'm a production environment message!"
    ```

    ❑ In `config/test.exs`, add the following:

    ```
    use Mix.Config
    ```

```
config :config_example,
  message_two: "I'm a test environment message!"
```

5. Define two module attributes in `lib/config_example.ex` to hold the values of `message_one` and `message_two`, as follows:

```
@message_one Application.get_env(:config_example, :message_one)
@message_two Application.get_env(:config_example, :message_two)
```

6. Create a `show_messages` function in `lib/config_example.ex`, like this:

```
def show_messages do
  IO.puts "Message one is: #{@message_one}"
  IO.puts "Message two is: #{@message_two}"
end
```

7. Start the application in the three different environments and see the output of the `show_messages` function:

   ❏ For the development environment, start the application as follows:

```
> MIX_ENV=dev iex -S mix

iex(1)> ConfigExample.show_messages

Message one is: This is a shared message!

Message two is: I'm a development environment message!

:ok

iex(2)>
```

   ❏ For the production environment, start the application like this:

```
> MIX_ENV=prod iex -S mix

iex(1)> ConfigExample.show_messages

Message one is: This is a shared message!

Message two is: I'm a production environment message!

:ok

iex(2)>
```

   ❏ For the test environment, start the application as follows:

```
> MIX_ENV=test iex -S mix

iex(1)> ConfigExample.show_messages

Message one is: This is a shared message!

Message two is: I'm a test environment message!

:ok

iex(2)>
```

How it works...

When we include the last line in `config.exs` (`import_config "#{Mix.env}.exs"`), the Mix configuration is loaded from the files, in this case with the Mix environment as its name and `.exs` as its extension.

The configuration from the imported files will override any existing configuration (with the same key) in the `config.exs` file. In fact, Configuration values are merged recursively. See the example at `https://github.com/alco/mix-config-example`.

To access configuration values, we use `Application.get_env(:app, :key)`.

Creating custom Mix tasks

Sometimes, the existing Mix tasks just aren't enough. Fortunately, Mix allows the creation of customized tasks that integrate as if they were shipped with Mix itself. In this recipe, we will create a custom Mix task that will print the Erlang VM memory status.

How to do it...

The steps required to create a custom task are as follows:

1. Create a new file, `meminfo.ex`, that defines the `Meminfo` module inside `Mix.Tasks`:

```
defmodule Mix.Tasks.Meminfo do
  use Mix.Task
end
```

2. Add the new task description to be displayed when `mix help` is invoked:

```
@shortdoc "Get Erlang VM memory usage information"
```

3. Add the new task module documentation:

```
@moduledoc """
A mix custom task that outputs some information regarding
the Erlang VM memory usage
"""
```

4. Create a `run/1` function:

```
def run(_) do
  meminfo = :erlang.memory
  IO.puts """
  Total            #{meminfo[:total]}
```

```
        Processes           #{meminfo[:processes]}
        Processes (used) #{meminfo[:processes_used]}
        System              #{meminfo[:system]}
        Atom                #{meminfo[:atom]}
        Atom (used)         #{meminfo[:atom_used]}
        Binary              #{meminfo[:binary]}
        Code                #{meminfo[:code]}
        ETS                 #{meminfo[:ets]}
        """
    end
```

5. Compile the code using the Elixir compiler, `elixirc`:

    elixirc meminfo.ex

    No message should appear but a file named `Elixir.Mix.Tasks.Meminfo.beam` is created.

6. Run `mix help` to see the new task listed and its short description:

    ```
    > mix help
    mix                 # Run the default task (current: mix run)
    mix archive         # List all archives
    (...)
    mix meminfo      # Get Erlang VM memory usage information
    mix new             # Create a new Elixir project
    mix run             # Run the given file or expression
    mix test            # Run a project's tests
    iex -S mix          # Start IEx and run the default task
    ```

7. Execute the custom task:

    ```
    > mix meminfo
    Total               17692216
    Processes           4778984
    Processes (used) 4777656
    System              12913232
    Atom                339441
    Atom (used)         321302
    Binary              14152
    Code                8136817
    ETS                 452832
    ```

How it works...

Mix tasks are just modules that are declared as `Mix.Tasks.<MODULENAME>` with a `run` function defined.

In `meminfo.ex`, we use the `Mix.Task` module by declaring `use Mix.Task`. The `use` directive allows us to use a given module in the current context.

The `@shortdoc` attribute allows us to define a short description to display when some help on Mix or the `mix.task` is displayed.

The `run/1` function is the place where all of the task's work is done. In this particular case, we use an Erlang function to return a keyword list with several entries, and print them for the user in a formatted way.

2
Data Types and Structures

This chapter will cover the following recipes:

- ▶ Understanding immutability
- ▶ Adding and subtracting lists
- ▶ Combining tuples into a list
- ▶ Creating and manipulating keyword lists
- ▶ Using pattern matching
- ▶ Pattern matching an HTTPoison response
- ▶ Creating a key/value store with a map
- ▶ Mapping and reducing enumerables
- ▶ Generating lazy (even infinite) sequences
- ▶ Streaming a file as a resource

Understanding immutability

In Elixir, data, once created, is immutable. Whenever some input is passed into a function to be transformed, the original value remains unchanged and a new value is created.

This allows for safe concurrent access to the same data by *n* processes. It makes concurrency easier to manage, as it is guaranteed that no process can change the original data. Any transformation on the original data will result in new data being created.

Getting ready

To get started, we need to follow these steps:

1. Create a file, which is `transformator.ex`, defining the `Transformator` module by adding the following code:

```
defmodule Transformator do
  @default_list [1,2,3,4,5,6]

  def get_odd_numbers(list \\ @default_list) do
    Enum.filter(list, fn(x)-> rem(x,2) == 1 end)
  end

  def get_even_numbers(list \\ @default_list) do
    Enum.filter(list, fn(x)-> rem(x,2) == 0 end)
  end
end
```

 We define `@default_list` and use it in both functions preceded by `\\`. This means that, if no argument is passed into the functions, they will behave as if we have passed the list [1,2,3,4,5,6].

2. Start an IEx session in your console:

   `>iex`

3. Compile the `Transformator` module:

   `iex(1)> c("transformator.ex")`

   `[Transformator]`

 It is possible to start IEx and compile the module in one step. To do so, replace steps 2 and 3 with the following command:

`iex transformator.ex`

How to do it...

To demonstrate the immutability of data, we will follow these steps using our IEx session:

1. Create a list called `original`:

   `iex(2)> original = [1, 2, 3, 4, 5, 6, 7, 8, 9]`

2. Pass the `original` list into the `get_odd_numbers` function of `Transformator`, assigning the result to `odd`:

```
iex(.3)> odd = Transformator.get_odd_numbers(original)
[1, 3, 5, 7, 9]
```

3. Pass the `original` list into the `get_even_numbers` function of `Transformator`, assigning the result to `even`:

```
iex(4)> even = Transformator.get_even_numbers(original)
[2, 4, 6, 8]
```

4. Apply the `foldl` function to the `odd`, `even`, and `original` lists to return the sum of all elements in each list:

```
iex(5)> List.foldl(original, 0, fn (x, acc) -> x + acc end)
45
iex(6)> List.foldl(odd, 0, fn (x, acc) -> x + acc end)
25
iex(7)> List.foldl(even, 0, fn (x, acc) -> x + acc end)
20
```

The `List.foldl/3` function reduces the given list towards the left with a function. We pass the list we want to reduce, an accumulator, and the function we wish to apply.

In this case, we pass each of the lists, an accumulator with the initial value of 0, and sum each element of the list with the accumulator.

5. We will now take each of the lists and shuffle them to change the order of their elements:

```
iex(8)> Enum.shuffle(original)
[3, 7, 2, 8, 6, 4, 9, 1, 5]
iex(9)> Enum.shuffle(odd)
[7, 1, 5, 9, 3]
iex(10)> Enum.shuffle(even)
[2, 6, 8, 4]
```

6. Verify each list to see that it has not changed:

```
iex(11)> even
[2, 4, 6, 8]
iex(12)> odd
[1, 3, 5, 7, 9]
iex(13)> original
[1, 2, 3, 4, 5, 6, 7, 8, 9]
```

How it works...

In steps 2 and 3, we pass our data structure (the `original` list) into functions that filter that data structure, and in step 4, we take our lists and reduce them by summing all their values. All these transformations occur without changing any of the original data. In step 5, immutability becomes clearer as we actually pass the lists into a function that potentially changes the order of its elements and yet that change is made by taking the original data, copying it, and creating new lists. As we can see in the final step, the input data has not changed.

If you use values greater than 65 in the input lists for the functions defined in the `Transformator` module, you might be surprised with the output you get in IEx. You could try the following:

```
iex(1)> Transformator.get_even_numbers
  ([65,66,67,68,69,70])
'BDF'
```

The output, which is BDF, is IEx interpreting the resulting list [66, 68, 70] as a character list, where 66 is the ASCII value for B, 68 for D, and 70 for F.

Adding and subtracting lists

Lists are widely used in functional programming languages, and Elixir is no exception.

Although lists might resemble other languages' arrays, they actually behave more like single-linked lists. Operations with lists are quite common, so in this recipe, we will show you how to add two lists or subtract one list from another.

Getting ready

We will use IEx for this recipe, so start a new session by typing `iex` in your console.

How to do it...

To add lists, we will use the `++` operator. The steps are as follows:

1. Create a list named `list_one`:

   ```
   iex(1)> list_one = [1, 3, 5]
   [1, 3, 5]
   ```

2. Create a list named `list_two`:

   ```
   iex(2)> list_two = [2, 4, 6, 5]
   [2, 4, 6, 5]
   ```

3. Add `list_one` to `list_two`:

   ```
   iex(3)> list_one ++ list_two
   [1, 3, 5, 2, 4, 6, 5]
   ```

4. Add `list_two` to `list_one`:

   ```
   iex(4)> list_two ++ list_one
   [2, 4, 6, 5, 1, 3, 5]
   ```

To subtract lists, we will be using the `--` operator:

1. Create a list named `list_three`:

   ```
   iex(5)> list_three = [1, 2, 3, 4, 5, 7, 8, 9]
   [1, 2, 3, 4, 5, 7, 8, 9]
   ```

2. Create a list named `list_four`:

   ```
   iex(6)> list_four = [2, 4, 6]
   [2, 4, 6]
   ```

3. Subtract `list_three` from `list_four`:

   ```
   iex(7)> list_three -- list_four
   [1, 3, 5, 7, 8, 9]
   ```

4. Subtract `list_four` from `list_three`:

   ```
   iex(8)> list_four -- list_three
   [6]
   ```

How it works...

The `++` operator appends each element of the right-hand side operand list to the left-hand side operand list.

The `--` operator removes the elements of the right-hand side operand list that exist in the left-hand side operand list. If we inspect the result in step 4, we can see that the values 2 and 4 exist in both lists; hence, they are removed from `list_four`, which keeps 6 as its only element, as it does not exist in `list_three`.

Combining tuples into a list

Elixir has a tuple data type. A tuple, like a list, can contain different types at the same time but guarantees that its elements are stored contiguously in memory.

Tuples are declared using brackets ({ }) and are often used as function return values and in-function pattern matching.

Getting ready

In this recipe, we will be using an IEx session. Start it by executing `iex` in your console.

How to do it...

We will create two tuples, one with **atoms** and one with **integers**, and then we will combine them. To do so, we need to convert them into lists:

1. Create `tuple_one`:

    ```
    iex(1)> tuple_one = {:one, :two, :three}
    {:one, :two, :three}
    ```

2. Create `tuple_two`:

    ```
    iex(2)> tuple_two = {1, 2, 3, 4}
    {1, 2, 3, 4}
    ```

3. Try to interpolate these two tuples by combining each value on the *nth* position of `tuple_one` with the *nth* value of `tuple_two`. We will be using the `Enum.zip/2` function:

    ```
    iex(3)> Enum.zip(tuple_one,tuple_two)
    ** (Protocol.UndefinedError) protocol Enumerable not implemented
    for {:one, :two, :three}
    ```

     `Enum.zip/2` takes two collections and zips corresponding elements into a list of tuples.

4. We need to convert the tuples into lists before combining them. Let's do the conversion and combining in one step:

    ```
    iex(3)> Enum.zip(Tuple.to_list(tuple_one), Tuple.to_list(tuple_two))
    [one: 1, two: 2, three: 3]
    ```

5. Let's make sure the result we got in the previous step is, in fact, a list:

```
iex(4)> Enum.zip(Tuple.to_list(tuple_one), Tuple.to_list(tuple_
two)) |> is_list
true
```

How it works...

Tuples are a convenient way to store, normally, two or three associated values. However, adding values to tuples is an expensive operation as it implies copying the entire structure. When we need to combine values from two different tuples, before interpolating them, it is more convenient to construct a list.

In step 3, we tried to use a function from the `Enum` module to combine both tuples and we got an error (a protocol-undefined error) as the tuples are not treated as collections and they don't implement the `Enumerable` protocol.

In step 4, we passed `Tuple.to_list(tuple_one)` and `Tuple.to_list(tuple_two)` as arguments to the `Enum.zip` function. The `Tuple.to_list/1` function transforms a tuple into a list. As both tuples were converted, it allowed us to combine them using `Enum.zip` because lists implement the `Enumerable` protocol.

The resulting list (`[one: 1, two: 2, three: 3]`) is, in fact, a list of tuples also known as a **keyword list**.

In step 5, we used the pipe operator (`|>`) to feed the result of the left-hand side expression as the first argument of the `is_list` function.

> The `Enum.zip/2` function takes two collections and zips corresponding elements into a list of tuples. In this task, `tuple_one` had three elements and as `tuple_two` had four, no corresponding value existed. Therefore, the last element (4) got discarded.

See also

▶ In the next recipe, *Creating and manipulating keyword lists*, we will be looking into keyword lists.

Creating and manipulating keyword lists

Tuples are often used to represent associative data structures. In Elixir, a list of two element tuples whose first element is an atom is called a keyword list.

Keyword lists have some particular features:

▸ They maintain the order of the elements as defined when creating and adding elements

▸ They allow repeated keys

Getting ready

Start a new IEx session by entering `iex` in your command line.

How to do it...

We will follow these steps to create and manipulate keyword lists:

1. Create a list with three tuples:

```
iex(1)> t1 = {:jane, 23}
iex(2)> t2 = {:jill, 44}
iex(3)> t3 = {:joe, 32}
iex(4)> kw_list = [t1, t2, t3]
[jane: 23, jill: 44, joe: 32]
```

2. Add a new entry at the end of the list:

```
iex(5)> kw_list = kw_list ++ [anthony: 22]
[jane: 23, jill: 44, joe: 32, anthony: 22]
```

3. Add a new entry at the beginning of the list:

```
iex(6)> kw_list = [zoe: 28] ++ kw_list
[zoe: 28, jane: 23, jill: 44, joe: 32, anthony: 22]
```

4. Add an already existing key to the list:

```
iex(7)> kw_list = kw_list ++ [jill: 19]
[zoe: 28, jane: 23, jill: 44, joe: 32, anthony: 22, jill: 19]
```

5. Remove an entry from the list:

```
iex(8)> kw_list = kw_list -- [joe: 32]
[zoe: 28, jane: 23, jill: 44, anthony: 22, jill: 19]
```

6. Sort the keyword list:

```
iex(9)> Enum.sort(kw_list)
[anthony: 22, jane: 23, jill: 19, jill: 44, zoe: 28]
```

7. Retrieve a value from the list:

```
iex(10)> kw_list[:jill]
44
```

How it works...

In step 1, when creating a list of tuples with an atom as their first element, a keyword list is returned.

Steps 2 and 3 exemplify the appending and prepending of new elements in a keyword list using the ++ operator. Notice that elements maintain the declared order. Keys are not sorted.

If an element with a different format is added to the list, that is, if it doesn't comply with the [:atom, value] form, the returned list will no longer be a keyword list. Let's look at an example:

iex(11)> kw_list ++ [:james]

[{:zoe, 28}, {:jane, 23}, {:jill, 44}, {:anthony, 22},
  {:jill, 19}, :james]

Keyword lists support repeated occurrences of a key. In step 4, the inserted key already existed in the keyword list, but it was inserted nonetheless.

The -- operator can also be used in keyword lists. Step 5 illustrates how it is possible to remove a given key/value pair from the keyword list.

To remove a key/value pair from a keyword list, both the key and the value must match. Let's try to remove a nonexisting key/value pair:

iex(12)> kw_list
[zoe: 28, jane: 23, jill: 44, anthony: 22, jill: 19]
iex(13)> kw_list -- [jane: 22]
[zoe: 28, jane: 23, jill: 44, anthony: 22, jill: 19]
Nothing was removed!

As mentioned earlier, keyword lists' elements maintain the declared order. However, this doesn't mean we cannot choose to sort the keyword list. In step 6, the Enum.sort/1 function is used to do this. Sorting takes the keys into account and only if they repeat their values will they be used as additional sorting criteria.

Note that in step 6, we performed the sorting without rebinding the result to kw_list. As we can see in the *Understanding immutability* recipe, data is immutable, so the keyword list we used in step 7 is not sorted!

A value for a given key can be retrieved using the list[:key] syntax. The returned value, if repeated keys exist, will be the first value found; for example, in step 7 the returned value is the first value found even though there is a smaller value under the :jill key.

Using pattern matching

In some of the previous recipes, we've been using the = operator. When we execute something like a = 1, we are not performing an assignment; we are, instead, binding the value 1 to a.

This is actually pattern matching in its simplest form. The = operator is, in fact, called the match operator.

Getting ready

Start a new IEx session in your console.

How to do it...

To exercise our pattern matching techniques, we will follow these steps:

1. Let's create a keyword list with our friends' birthdays:

   ```
   iex(1)> birthday_list = [andrew: "October 2nd", jim: "May 1st",
   carrie: "September 23rd", Carla: "August 30th"]

   [andrew: "October 2nd", jim: "May 1st", carrie: "September
   23rd",carla: "August 30th"]
   ```

2. Now, we will be getting the first element of the list (also known as head of the list):

   ```
   iex(2)> [head|tail] = birthday_list

   [andrew: "October 2nd", jim: "May 1st", carrie: "September
   23rd",carla: "August 30th"]

   iex(3)> head

   {:andrew, "October 2nd"}
   ```

3. All the other values (the tail of the list) are bound to the tail variable:

   ```
   iex(4)> tail

   [jim: "May 1st", carrie: "September 23rd", carla: "August 30th"]
   ```

4. Let's get the head of the tail! Confusing? Think of the tail as a list and we will get the first element of that list:

   ```
   iex(5)> [tail_head|tail_tail] = tail

   [jim: "May 1st", carrie: "September 23rd", carla: "August 30th"]
   ```

```
iex(6)> tail_head
{:jim, "May 1st"}
```

5. Sometimes while performing pattern matching, some values do not interest us. We will get the first element of our birthday list and ignore all the other elements:

```
iex(7)> [first_friend|_] = birthday_list
[andrew: "October 2nd", jim: "May 1st", carrie: "September 23rd",
carla: "August 30th"]
iex(8)> first_friend
{:andrew, "October 2nd"}
```

6. Now, let's try to access the _ variable from our previous match:

```
iex(9)> _
** (CompileError) iex:9: unbound variable _
```

7. How about getting the birthday of the first friend in the list? Take a look:

```
iex(10)> [{_, day}|t] = birthday_list
[andrew: "October 2nd", jim: "May 1st", carrie: "September 23rd",
carla: "August 30th"]
iex(11)> day
"October 2nd"
```

How it works...

We started by defining a keyword list just like we did in the *Creating and manipulating keyword lists* recipe.

In step 2, we pattern matched our `birthday_list` into `head` and `tail`. The `head` variable is the first element of our keyword list and `tail` contains all other elements. If we take a closer look, `head` is a tuple and `tail` is a keyword list. We checked the `tail` variable's contents in step 3.

Lists are recursively defined, so in step 4, we pattern match again. However, this time, instead of using the original `birthday_list`, we use `tail`. This time, `tail_head` is, in fact, the second element of the original `birthday_list`.

Step 5 illustrates the use of a "don't care" variable (_). We use this when the values matched are not of any interest to us. It is kind of a black hole where we send data that we don't care about.

In the example, we got the first element of the list. What if we want to get the second as well? Lists are a structure that can be defined recursively. If we think about it, then the second element of the list will be the first of the tail! Let's take a look at how to do it:

```
iex(14)> [first|[second|_]] = birthday_list
iex(15)> first
{:andrew, "October 2nd"}
iex(16)> second
{:jim, "May 1st"}
```

The final step shows you how it is possible to perform pattern matching inside another pattern matching.

As shown in step 2, the first element of our `birthday_list` is the tuple `{:andrew, "October 2nd"}`. As we were only interested in the day, we discarded the name with an underscore.

In step 7, we can get the day in a single operation. We could have done it in two steps like this:

```
iex(12)> [ first_element | _ ] = birthday_list
iex(13)> { _, day } = first_element
iex(14)> day
"October 2nd"
```

See also

▶ In the *Using guard clauses and pattern matching in function definitions* recipe of *Chapter 4, Modules and Functions*, we will be using pattern matching.

Pattern matching an HTTPoison response

HTTPoison is an HTTP client for Elixir. We have already used it in the *Managing dependencies* recipe of *Chapter 1, Command Line*.

In this recipe, we will create a simple application that will take a URL and fetch the corresponding page, returning either the body or the headers of that request.

Getting ready

We will be using the `get_pages` application. You will find it in the source code of this book. The steps are as follows:

1. Enter the application directory:

   ```
   > cd get_pages
   ```

2. Fetch the dependencies and compile them:

   ```
   > mix deps.get && mix deps.compile
   ```

3. Start the application:

   ```
   > iex -S mix
   ```

How to do it...

To get an HTTP response and perform pattern matching on it, we will follow these steps:

1. Issue a request to fetch the `elixir-lang` main page and take the headers from the response:

   ```
   iex(1)> GetPages.get(:headers, "http://elixir-lang.com")
   ```

   The result is shown in the following screenshot:

   ```
   Interactive Elixir (1.0.0) - press Ctrl+C to exit (type h() ENTER for help)
   iex(1)> GetPages.get(:headers, "http://elixir-lang.com")
   %{"Cache-Control" => "no-cache", "Connection" => "keep-alive",
     "Date" => "Thu, 18 Sep 2014 13:43:16 GMT",
     "Location" => "http://elixir-lang.org", "Server" => "nginx/1.4.1",
     "Status" => "302 Found", "Transfer-Encoding" => "chunked",
     "X-Rack-Cache" => "miss",
     "X-Request-Id" => "94ab0cc302a9a53d27a70f1e948dac61",
     "X-Runtime" => "0.003256", "X-UA-Compatible" => "IE=Edge,chrome=1"}
   iex(2)> _
   ```

2. Now, we will request the main Google page and take the body from the response:

   ```
   iex(2)> GetPages.get(:body, "https://www.google.com")
   ```

The result is shown in the following screenshot:

```
iex(2)> GetPages.get(:body, "https://www.google.com")
"<HTML><HEAD><meta http-equiv=\"content-type\" content=\"text/html;charset=utf-8\">\n<TITLE>3
82 Moved</TITLE></HEAD><BODY>\n<H1>302 Moved</H1>\nThe document has moved\n<A HREF=\"https://
www.google.pt/?gfe_rd=cr&amp;ei=seIaVJnaFOus8wfEg4CYCA\">here</A>.\r\n</BODY></HTML>\r\n"
iex(3)>
```

3. What if we try to get something other than the body or the headers from the response? Take a look:

   ```
   iex(3)> GetPages.get(:something, "http://elixir-lang.com")
   Section unavailable or not known!
   :ok
   ```

How it works...

To see pattern matching in action, open the get_pages/lib/get_pages.ex file, which has the following content:

```elixir
defmodule GetPages do

  def get(element, url \\ "http://elixir-lang.org") do
    case element do
      :headers ->
        %{headers: headers} = fetch_url(url)
        headers
      :body ->
        %{:body => body} = fetch_url(url)
        body
      _ ->
        IO.puts "Section unavailable or not known!"
    end
  end

  defp fetch_url(url)  do
    HTTPoison.get(url)
  end

end
```

We will start by examining the `fetch_url(url)` function. This function is defined with `defp` instead of `def`, which means that this function is private; it can only be invoked from within the `GetPages` module. It receives a string representing a URL and then invokes the `HTTPoison` app that we declared as a dependency. The return result is a map named `HTTPoison.Response`, containing body and headers keys.

The `fetch_url` function is invoked by the `get` function.

The `get` function accepts an atom to determine what section of the response we wish to retrieve (`:headers` or `:body`) and a string defining the desired page's URL.

> In the `def get(element, url \\ "http://elixir-lang.org")` function definition, we have `\\` after the URL. This is called a default argument. If no value is provided, the function will default to the one defined after `\\`.
>
> This means that `GetPages.get(:body, "http://elixir-lang.org")` is equivalent to `GetPages.get(:body)`.

Pattern matching takes place in the `case element do` section.

The **If** element matches `:headers`; we then retrieve the value under the `:headers` key in the response, assigning it to the `headers` variable and returning it.

The **Else if** element matches `:body`; we then retrieve the value under the `:body` key in the response, assigning it to the `body` variable and returning it.

The **Else** element was not captured in the previous matches, so we will issue a message to inform the user. The _ variable in pattern matching means that we don't care for the value and, in this case, it is a match-all operator.

Previously, we highlighted If, Else if, and Else to make clear that pattern matching actually replaces the need for these constructs!

Pattern matching also takes place in `%{:headers => headers} = fetch_url(url)` and `%{:body => body} = fetch_url(url)`. The `fetch_url(url)` function on the right-hand side of the match operator (`=`) returns a map, and by declaring a map (`%{}`) on the left-hand side of the match operator, we are taking only the `:headers` or `:body` key and assigning its value to a variable.

Creating a key/value store with a map

In Elixir, **map** is the tool to use when we need a very simple key/value store. A map is a data type for associative collections (or dictionaries).

The Map module is an implementation of the Dict API. The following is the Dict documentation page:

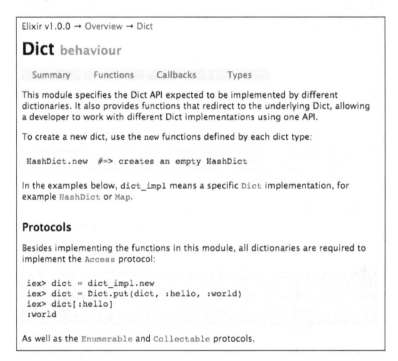

```
Elixir v1.0.0 → Overview → Dict
```

Dict behaviour

Summary   Functions   Callbacks   Types

This module specifies the Dict API expected to be implemented by different dictionaries. It also provides functions that redirect to the underlying Dict, allowing a developer to work with different Dict implementations using one API.

To create a new dict, use the new functions defined by each dict type:

```
HashDict.new   #=> creates an empty HashDict
```

In the examples below, dict_impl means a specific Dict implementation, for example HashDict or Map.

Protocols

Besides implementing the functions in this module, all dictionaries are required to implement the Access protocol:

```
iex> dict = dict_impl.new
iex> dict = Dict.put(dict, :hello, :world)
iex> dict[:hello]
:world
```

As well as the Enumerable and Collectable protocols.

Getting ready

Start a new IEx session in your console.

How to do it...

In this recipe, we will create an in-memory database of the English Premier League, where we will keep the current points, number of played games, and the club name. We will be creating a map to hold the league and a map for each team. This will be a map of maps! The steps are as follows:

1. We will create the map to hold the League data:

   ```
   iex(1)> premier_league_2013 = %{}
   ```

> To create a new map, we might also use the `Map.new/0` function:
> ```
> premier_league = Map.new
> ```

2. Now, it's time to add some data about the teams:

   ```
   iex(2)> man_city = %{:position=> 1, :points=> 86, :played=> 38,
   :name=> "Manchester City"}
   iex(3)> liverpool = %{:position => 2, :points=> 84, :played=> 38,
   :name=> "Liverpool"}
   iex(4)> chelsea = %{:position => 3, :points=> 82, :played=> 38,
   :name=> "Chelsea"}
   ```

3. We will now add the teams to our league map:

   ```
   iex(5)> premier_league_2013 = %{:man_city=> man_city, :liverpool
   => liverpool, :chelsea => chelsea}
   %{chelsea: %{name: "Chelsea", played: 38, points: 82, position:
   3},
      liverpool: %{name: "Liverpool", played: 38, points: 84,
   position: 2},
      man_city: %{name: "Manchester City", played: 38, points: 86,
   position: 1}}
   ```

4. Now, we will get the name and points stored in our league map with the Chelsea key assigning them to the n and p variables:

   ```
   iex(6)> %{:name => n, :points => p} =  Map.get(premier_
   league_2013, :chelsea)
   iex(7)> n
   "Chelsea"
   iex(8)> p
   82
   ```

How it works...

In step 1, we created a named map, and in the next step, we created maps to hold the information of three teams. The syntax we used is `%{:key => value}`.

We used the same syntax to put each team's map on our `premier_league_2013` map.

 We could have added each team into the league map using the `Map.put/3` function:

`premier_league_2013 = Map.put(premier_league_2013, :man_city, man_city)`

Repeat the procedure for each of the teams we want to add.

In the last step, we used pattern matching and the `Map.get/3` function to assign only the `name` and `points` values under the `:chelsea` key on our `premier_league_2013` map.

On the left-hand side of the match operator (`=`), we declared a map, assigning the `:name` key to the `n` variable and `:points` to the `p` variable.

Unlike keyword lists, maps don't maintain the order of the declared keys and they also don't allow duplicate entries under the same key.

See also

▶ We used pattern matching in this recipe. To see some examples of pattern matching, take a look at the *Using pattern matching* and *Pattern matching a HTTPoison response* recipes.

Mapping and reducing enumerables

In Elixir, protocols are a way to achieve polymorphism. The `Enum` and `Stream` modules work on data types that implement the `Enumerable` protocol, so the behavior of both modules becomes similar. In this context, polymorphism might be perceived as a common API to interact with different modules.

All `Enum` module functions accept a collection as one of the arguments, and two very common operations in collections are map and reduce. With map, we perform some kind of operation on every element of a given collection, and with reduce, the whole collection is reduced into a value.

Getting ready

For this recipe, we will use a new IEx session. To start it, type `iex` in your console.

How to do it...

To perform map and reduce on a collection, we will be following these steps:

1. We will start by creating a list with numbers from 1 to 9

   ```
   iex(1)> my_list = Enum.to_list(1..9)
   [1, 2, 3, 4, 5, 6, 7, 8, 9]
   ```

2. Create an anonymous function to map the collection:

   ```
   iex(2)> my_map_function_one = fn(x)-> x*x end
   #Function<6.90072148/1 in :erl_eval.expr/5>
   ```

3. Apply the function to every element of the collection:

   ```
   iex(3)> Enum.map(my_list, my_map_function_one)
   [1, 4, 9, 16, 25, 36, 49, 64, 81]
   ```

4. Let's create a map function that subtracts 1 from even numbers and adds 1 to odd numbers:

   ```
   iex(4)> my_map_function_two = fn(x)-> cond do
   ...(4)> rem(x,2)==0 ->
   ...(4)> x - 1
   ...(4)> rem(x,2)==1 ->
   ...(4)> x + 1
   ...(4)> end
   ...(4)> end
   #Function<6.90072148/1 in :erl_eval.expr/5>
   ```

5. Apply this map function to the list:

   ```
   iex(5)> Enum.map(my_list, my_map_function_two)
   [2, 1, 4, 3, 6, 5, 8, 7, 10]
   ```

6. To reduce our original list, we will create a reduce anonymous function:

   ```
   iex(5)> my_reduce_function = fn(x, acc)-> x + acc end
   #Function<12.90072148/2 in :erl_eval.expr/5>
   ```

7. Reduce the list by applying my_reduce_function:

   ```
   iex(6)> Enum.reduce(my_list, my_reduce_function)
   45
   ```

How it works...

After creating an initial collection to work on, we defined three anonymous functions in steps 2, 4, and 6. We could have passed the function definitions directly, but to make the examples clearer, we assigned these anonymous functions to variables.

In step 2, `my_map_function_one` takes a single input and multiplies that input by itself.

In step 4, `my_map_function_two` also takes a single input but uses `cond` to determine whether that input is an even or odd value. If the input is an even value, it will be decremented by one, and if the input is an odd number, it will be incremented by one.

The reduce function defined in step 6 (`my_reduce_function`) takes two inputs, a collection element (`x`), and an accumulator (`acc`). In this particular case, we are adding all elements of `my_list`, reducing them to a single value.

To map (steps 3 and 5) and reduce (step 7), we used functions from the `Enum` module as it implements the `Enumerable` protocol and allows us to work with any data structure that supports enumeration.

There is more...

In step 7, we chose the `Enum.reduce/2` function but we could have used `Enum.reduce/3`, which takes an extra argument that will be the accumulator. In `Enum.reduce/2`, the accumulator is the first element of the collection.

This is how we use the `Enum.reduce/3` function:

```
Enum.reduce(collection, accumulator, reduce_function)
iex(7)> Enum.reduce(my_list, 0, my_reduce_function)
45
```

In the *Understanding immutability* recipe, we used the `List.foldl/3` function to reduce the list. We could have used it here as we also had a list as our collection. However, by using the `reduce` function defined in the `Enum` module, we are able to use the same code even if the collection is not a list. This is polymorphism, and it is made possible by the use of protocols!

Generating lazy (even infinite) sequences

In the *Mapping and reducing enumerables* recipe, we made use of the `Enum` module. In this recipe, we will be using the `Stream` module.

While `Enum` functions are all eager, in `Stream`, they are lazy.

Let's inspect the following code:

```
Enum.to_list(1..1000000) |> Enum.map(&(&1 * &1)) |> Enum.sum
```

This code is performing a sequence of operations using the `Enum` module. All steps between the pipe operators (`|>`) imply the calculation of the entire data structures and placing them in memory. A list with numbers from 1 to 1000000 is created, then a new list containing each of the previous elements multiplied by themselves is created, and finally, this resulting list is reduced by summing up all elements.

This is an example of eager evaluation. What if we wish to work with data that doesn't fit in our available memory?

How to do it...

To work with enumerables and lazy evaluate them, we will follow these steps:

1. Start an IEx session.
2. Define an **enumerable**:

   ```
   iex(1)> collection = 1..10000000
   1..10000000
   ```

3. Perform several transformations on the collection created in the previous step using the `Stream` module:

   ```
   iex(2)> my_stream = 1..10000000 |>
   ...(2)> Stream.filter_map((&(rem(&1,13)==0)), (&(&1*&1))) |>
   ...(2)> Stream.filter(&(rem(&1,2)==1))
   #Stream<[enum: 1..10000000,
    funs: [#Function<59.45151713/1 in Stream.filter_map/3>,
      #Function<38.45151713/1 in Stream.filter/2>]]>
   ```

4. Let's now reduce our *collection* by summing its values:

   ```
   iex(3)> my_stream |> Enum.sum
   12820474358991153855
   ```

How it works...

In step 1, we defined a range with all the integers between 1 (first) and 10000000 (last).

 We could have used `Range.new(first, last)`:
```
iex(4)> Range.new(1,10000000)
1..10000000
```

In step 2, we assigned a stream that resulted from several transformations in the `my_stream` variable. This resulting stream is lazy evaluated. Think of it as a series of computational directives waiting to be performed.

We will now take a closer look at each transformation:

- The first one, which uses `Stream.filter_map(enum, filter, mapper)`, selects each element of `my_stream` that is divisible by 13 and multiplies it by itself:
  - Our enum is the range of `1..10000000`
  - The filter function (`&(rem(&1,13)==0)`) chooses all elements from the collection that are divisible by 13
  - The map function (`&(&1*&1)`) multiplies the element by itself

- The next one, which is `Stream.filter(enum, function)`, selects every odd element from the `Stream` resulting from the previous transformation:
  - The enum parameter is the `Stream` returned by the previous transformation
  - The filter function (`&(rem(&1,2)==1)`) selects every odd element

To sum it all, we are taking all numbers from 1 to 10000000, selecting the ones divisible by 13 and multiplying them by themselves and then filtering the resulting collection to select only the odd ones. At this stage, no computation was actually performed! We get the following return value:

```
#Stream<[enum: 1..10000000, funs: [#Function<59.45151713/1 in Stream.
filter_map/3>, #Function<38.45151713/1 in Stream.filter/2>]]>
```

This is a lazy evaluated value.

Only in the final step, when we use `Enum.sum(collection)`, is the computation performed and we get the resulting sum of all elements from the `Stream` resulting from the previous transformations.

There is more...

As we used the `Stream` module instead of `Enum`, no intermediary values were generated in the transformations. Memory usage was reduced and we could have used a larger initial collection without worrying about maxing out the available memory.

The next two screenshots show you the memory usage by using lazy and eager evaluation.

Using lazy evaluation, we can do the following:

```
iex(5)> my_stream = 1..10000000 |>
...(5)> Stream.filter_map((&(rem(&1,13)==0)), (&(&1*&1))) |>
...(5)> Stream.filter(&(rem(&1,2)==1))
#Stream<[enum: 1..10000000,
```

```
funs: [#Function<60.29647706/1 in Stream.filter_map/3>,
    #Function<39.29647706/1 in Stream.filter/2>]]>
```

The transformation was defined but not yet executed. Take a look at the following:

```
iex(6)> my_stream |> Enum.sum
12820474358991153855
```

When we execute the preceding command, we get the following memory usage:

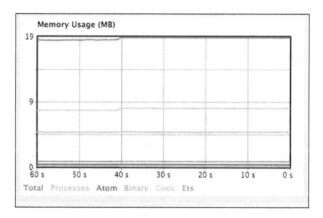

Replacing Stream with Enum using eager evaluation leads to the following:

```
iex(6)> my_stream = 1..10000000 |>
...(6)> Enum.filter_map((&(rem(&1,13)==0)), (&(&1*&1))) |>
...(6)> Enum.filter(&(rem(&1,2)==1)) |> Enum.sum
12820474358991153855
```

We have the following memory usage:

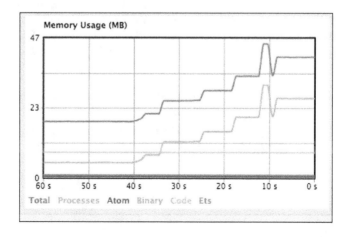

> The & (&1*&2) syntax used in this recipe's map and filter functions is a
> shortcut equivalent to using fn(x,y) -> x * y end, where & is fn
> and &1, &2, and &n are the 1st, 2nd, and nth arguments.

Streaming a file as a resource

In the *Generating lazy (even infinite) sequences* recipe, it was possible to understand the difference between eager and lazy evaluation, namely the use of Enum or Stream modules.

When working with files, it is possible to load all of the file's contents into the memory (File.read/1 or File.read!/1), or the file might be read a line or n bytes at a time (File.stream!/3). Using the File.stream! function allows you to work with really large files that might not fit the available memory.

In this recipe, we will read text from a file and output an uppercased version into a new file.

Getting ready

Start an IEx session and make sure you have stream_file.txt in a known location:

```
> iex
```

How to do it...

To read a file one line at a time (that is, streaming it), we will perform the following steps:

1. First, let's get information about the file we will be loading:

    ```
    iex(1)> File.stat("<path_to_file>/stream_file.txt")
    ```

    ```
    %File.Stat{access: :read_write, atime: {{2014, 9, 20}, {0,
    44, 19}}, ctime: {{2014, 9, 20}, {0, 44, 19}}, gid: 20, inode:
    34849976, links: 1, major_device: 16777218, minor_device: 0, mode:
    33188, mtime: {{2014, 9, 20}, {0, 44, 19}}, size: 8472, type:
    :regular, uid: 501}
    ```

2. Lazily read the file into the input_file variable:

    ```
    iex(2)> input_file = File.stream!("<path_to_file>/stream_file.
    txt")
    ```

    ```
    %File.Stream{line_or_bytes: :line, modes: [:raw, :read_ahead,
    :binary], path: "code/stream_file.txt", raw: true}
    ```

It is easier if you start the IEx session in the directory where `stream_file.txt` is stored. To load it, the filename is enough and the full (or relative) path is not needed:

```
iex(3)> input_file = File.stream!("stream_file.txt")
```

3. Perform the transformations that will make every letter uppercase and output the result into a new file:

```
iex(4)> input_file |>
...(4)> Stream.map(&String.upcase(&1)) |>
...(4)> Stream.into(File.stream!("code/new.txt")) |>
...(4)> Stream.run
:ok
```

4. Open the created `new.txt` file to see the result of our transformation:

```
⬤ ⬤ ⬤                        📄 new.txt
LOREM IPSUM DOLOR SIT AMET, CONSECTETUR ADIPISCING ELIT. UT FINIBUS ENIM NEC CONSEQUAT
INTERDUM. ALIQUAM UT PORTA ORCI. SUSPENDISSE A MAGNA VEL JUSTO TEMPUS SAGITTIS. QUISQUE AT
MOLESTIE IPSUM. QUISQUE PORTA SED NIBH EU SAGITTIS. QUISQUE SODALES CONSECTETUR VELIT
VITAE SUSCIPIT. DONEC EU ALIQUET LECTUS, ID BIBENDUM EROS. MAURIS SUSCIPIT DIAM AC LIGULA
EFFICITUR VENENATIS. ALIQUAM EU SAPIEN TORTOR. NUNC PELLENTESQUE TORTOR UT LIBERO POSUERE,
GRAVIDA TINCIDUNT NISI TEMPOR. MAURIS ULLAMCORPER MAURIS ET DIAM AUCTOR VULPUTATE. QUISQUE
BIBENDUM MATTIS TINCIDUNT. CUM SOCIIS NATOQUE PENATIBUS ET MAGNIS DIS PARTURIENT MONTES,
NASCETUR RIDICULUS MUS.
PRAESENT PORTTITOR VEL TORTOR AC ALIQUET. NUNC METUS SEM, LUCTUS NON VIVERRA EGET, MATTIS
VEL NIBH. VIVAMUS ELEIFEND FELIS UT CONDIMENTUM PORTTITOR. MAECENAS VULPUTATE RUTRUM EST A
GRAVIDA. ALIQUAM TINCIDUNT LOREM UT NISL TINCIDUNT FACILISIS. FUSCE EU TORTOR AT ODIO
VENENATIS MOLESTIE SIT AMET AT EX. INTEGER PHARETRA EX SIT AMET MAGNA DICTUM COMMODO.
UT HENDRERIT DUI A TEMPUS MOLLIS. SED LOREM LIGULA, ULLAMCORPER NEC IACULIS EGET, VOLUTPAT
AC FELIS. MORBI NON TELLUS SUSCIPIT, VEHICULA ODIO ID, EFFICITUR MI. PROIN FACILISIS VEL
LECTUS AC AUCTOR. ALIQUAM AC ORNARE ERAT, EU MALESUADA ENIM. PHASELLUS CONSECTETUR NULLA
NON MAGNA PULVINAR PULVINAR. DUIS RUTRUM IN ELIT QUIS LAOREET. NULLAM NEC FAUCIBUS MAGNA.
MORBI SAGITTIS SED TORTOR SIT AMET SUSCIPIT. ALIQUAM TELLUS METUS, PLACERAT AT MALESUADA
VEL, DIGNISSIM MAXIMUS TELLUS.
PELLENTESQUE LIGULA IPSUM, MOLLIS EGET GRAVIDA POSUERE, AUCTOR ID MI. FUSCE METUS SAPIEN,
MATTIS AT PELLENTESQUE A, ACCUMSAN VITAE EROS. QUISQUE SODALES, LIGULA EU VARIUS
CONSEQUAT, LECTUS DOLOR ALIQUAM DUI, NEC ELEMENTUM NEQUE RISUS CURSUS MAURIS. ETIAM MAGNA
METUS, FRINGILLA SIT AMET QUAM EGET, FRINGILLA SUSCIPIT NIBH. DONEC BLANDIT MI FRINGILLA,
DAPIBUS ELIT NON, PORTTITOR PURUS. CRAS AUCTOR MATTIS PELLENTESQUE. NULLA LACINIA FELIS
PURUS, NEC PULVINAR LECTUS TEMPOR EGET. SED NEC NEQUE NISL. MAECENAS FRINGILLA, LIGULA UT
FRINGILLA FACILISIS, FELIS EST RUTRUM DUI, ET SAGITTIS MAGNA EST AC TURPIS. MAURIS PRETIUM
ODIO NON MI LAOREET, VEL ULLAMCORPER NISI POSUERE. DONEC MAXIMUS TURPIS AT RISUS EFFICITUR
VARIUS. DONEC NUNC VELIT, CURSUS UT FERMENTUM EGET, ULTRICES A METUS. PRAESENT FINIBUS
PLACERAT LOREM, UT FAUCIBUS DOLOR.
NUNC MI EST, TEMPUS UT EGESTAS NON, HENDRERIT ID MAURIS. VIVAMUS SCELERISQUE CONGUE
SCELERISQUE. PROIN LACINIA NISL IN ARCU INTERDUM ULTRICIES. CRAS SIT AMET ELEMENTUM AUGUE.
```

How it works...

After checking the file information, we load the file into the `input_file` variable in step 2. The `File.stream!` function returns `File.Stream` and nothing is yet loaded into the memory!

In step 3, we pass `input_file` as the first argument to the `Stream.map` function along with the map function (`&String.upcase(&1)`) that converts every element of `input_file` to uppercase. Afterwards, the result of this mapping is passed as the first argument of the `Stream.into` function, which also takes a path indicating the file where the data will be written. At this point, no computation has taken place! Only in the last stage of our transformation (`Stream.run`) does the computation take place, resulting in the creation of a new file. At the end of our pipeline, `new.txt` is created, which is an uppercased version of `stream_file.txt`.

3
Strings and Binaries

This chapter will cover the following recipes:

- ▸ Joining strings
- ▸ Splitting strings
- ▸ Replacing string codepoints with patterns
- ▸ Slicing strings with ranges
- ▸ Using regular expressions
- ▸ Combining operations with the | > operator
- ▸ Creating a word list
- ▸ Determining the word frequency in a text
- ▸ Reading and writing metadata from MP3 files

Introduction

In Elixir, strings are declared using double quotes ("") and they are, by default, UTF-8-encoded binaries. A group of bytes represent each codepoint in a string.

 A codepoint, in this context, is the binary representation of a UTF-8-encoded character.

Elixir's support for strings is excellent. However, remember that under the hood, they are binaries!

In order to represent some characters in UTF-8, more than one byte is needed sometimes. Take a look at the following examples:

```
iex> byte_size "aeiou"
5
iex> byte_size "àéíôù"
10
iex> String.length "aeiou"
5
iex> String.length "àéíôù"
5
```

Even though both strings have the same length, the number of bytes needed to represent them differs.

Joining strings

As we mentioned in the introduction, strings are binaries. In this recipe, we will use the binary concatenation operator (<>) to join strings.

Getting ready

In this recipe, we will use an IEx session, so let's start it by entering `iex` in our command line.

How to do it...

To join (concatenate) two strings, follow these steps:

1. Define `string_one`:

```
iex(1)> string_one = "Hello"
"Hello"
```

2. Define `string_two`:

```
iex(2)> string_two = "World"
"World"
```

3. Join both strings:

```
iex(3)> string_one <> string_two
"HelloWorld"
```

4. Make it look a lot better:

```
iex(4)> string_one <> " " <> string_two <> "!"
"Hello World!"
```

How it works...

The `Kernel` module defines a macro to concatenate two binaries. Think of this macro as a `<>` operator that works by appending the binary defined on the right-hand side to the binary defined on the left-hand side. In step 3, we used previously defined strings and concatenated them using `<>`.

The operation is associative. In step 4, we concatenated a space and `!` to our defined strings using `<>` in a sequence.

There's more...

Elixir strings also support interpolation. By using `#{variable}`, we can insert some computed values into strings!

We can interpolate an x value into a string by defining it like this:

```
iex> x = 5
5
iex> "My x value is #{x} !"
"My x value is 5 !"
```

Many IO functions support iolists. If we wish to output the result of our concatenation using `IO.puts`, we can avoid concatenation and pass a list literal to the output function. Using iolists is faster and, most of the time, more memory-efficient.

To output the string defined in step 4 using an iolist, do the following:

```
iex(5)> IO.puts [string_one, " ", string_two, "!"]
Hello World!.
```

Splitting strings

Functions to work on strings are defined under the `String` module. In the next few recipes, we will be using some of these functions.

In this recipe, we will be focusing on how to split strings using `String.split/1`, `String.split/3` and `String.split_at/2`.

Getting ready

Start a new IEx session by typing `iex` in your command line.

How to do it...

To demonstrate the use of the `split` functions in the `String` module, we will follow these steps:

1. Define a string to work with:

    ```
    iex(1)> my_string = "Elixir, testing 1,2,3! Testing!"
    "Elixir, testing 1,2,3! Testing!"
    ```

2. Split a string at the whitespaces:

    ```
    iex(2)> String.split(my_string)
    ["Elixir,", "testing", "1,2,3!", "Testing!"]
    ```

3. Split a string at a given character, in this case at `,`:

    ```
    iex(3)> String.split(my_string, ",")
    ["Elixir", " testing 1", "2", "3! Testing!"]
    ```

4. Split a string at a given character and limit the number of splits to be performed:

    ```
    iex(4)> String.split(my_string, ",", parts: 2)
    ["Elixir", " testing 1,2,3! Testing!"]
    ```

5. Split a string into two parts, starting at a given offset:

    ```
    iex(5)> String.split_at(my_string, 7)
    {"Elixir,", " testing 1,2,3! Testing!"}
    iex(6)> String.split_at(my_string, -8)
    {"Elixir, testing 1,2,3! ", "Testing!"}
    ```

How it works...

In this recipe, to split our defined `my_string`, we used several functions defined in the `String` module.

We will now take a closer look at each one of them:

► In step 2, we use `String.split/1`, which accepts a string argument and defines the split character as a whitespace (" ").

► In step 3, we pass both the strings we wish to split and the character to be used as the split token to `String.split/2`.

- In both these steps, the return value is a list of strings with the split character removed (" " in step 2 and "," in step 3).

- Step 4 illustrates `String.split/3` with the use of options. In this particular case, we determined that the input string must be split in two parts.

- In the last step, we use the `String.split_at` function. This function splits a string in two, returning a two element tuple with the two strings resulting from the split. It is possible to use both positive and negative integer values for the offset. If a negative value is passed, the position where the input string must be split is counted from the end.

If the split offset's (positive or negative) absolute value is bigger than the length of a string, the `String.split_at` function returns a tuple with an empty string as its first element (if a negative offset with an absolute value bigger than the length is passed) or a tuple with an empty string as its second element (if a positive offset value bigger than the length is passed).

To better illustrate this, take a look at these examples:

```
iex> String.split_at("Demo", 5)
{"Demo", ""}
iex> String.split_at("Demo", -5)
{"", "Demo"}
```

See also

- In the *Replacing string codepoints with patterns* and *Slicing strings with ranges* recipes, we will find alternate ways to split strings.

Replacing string codepoints with patterns

In this recipe, we will demonstrate how to replace codepoints in a string using a match pattern. We will use the `String.replace/4` function to help with this task.

A codepoint, in this context, is the binary representation of a UTF-8 encoded character.

Getting ready

This recipe will be performed inside an IEx session. Start it by executing the `iex` command in your command line.

How to do it...

To find a pattern in a string and replace it, follow these steps:

1. Define a string:

    ```
    iex(1)> my_string = "user1@server.domain user2@server.domain"
    "user1@server.domain user2@server.domain"
    ```

2. Define a string pattern to use with `String.replace`:

    ```
    iex(2)> my_pattern = "@"
    "@"
    ```

3. Perform the replacement using the default options:

    ```
    iex(3)> String.replace(my_string, my_pattern, "(at)")
    "user1(at)server.domain user2(at)server.domain"
    ```

4. Perform the replacement only at the first pattern occurrence:

    ```
    iex(4)> String.replace(my_string, my_pattern, "(at)", global:
    false)
    "user1(at)server.domain user2@server.domain"
    ```

5. Now, find the pattern you wish to replace and reinsert it in the resulting string:

    ```
    iex(5)> String.replace(my_string, my_pattern, "()", insert_
    replaced: 1)
    "user1(@)server.domain user2(@)server.domain"
    ```

How it works...

The `String.replace(subject, pattern, replacement, options \\ [])` function takes as its arguments the string to process (subject), a pattern, the codepoints (replacement) we wish to replace the pattern with, and some options. A new string is returned containing the changed codepoints. Let's take a closer look at each step:

▶ In steps 1 and 2, we defined both the string (subject) we wished to transform and the pattern we wish to find in that string.

▶ In step 3, the `String.replace` function was invoked without passing any options. The default value when options are not passed is `global: true`. This means that all occurrences of the given pattern will be replaced. In this case, all @ characters were replaced by (at).

▶ In step 4, we changed this behavior by setting the option as `global: false`. This resulted in only the first occurrence of the defined pattern @ being replaced.

▶ In step 5, we see another option in action. This time, the `insert_replaced: 1` option is used. With this option, we define that we want the replaced codepoints (pattern) to be inserted inside the replacement codepoints. The integer 1 represents the index where we wish the pattern to be inserted.

The `insert_replaced` function can also be defined as a list of integers. Let's run the step 5 example with `insert_replaced: [0,2]`:

```
iex(6)> String.replace(my_string, "@", "()", insert_
replaced: [0,2])
"user1@()@server.domain, user2@()@server.domain"
```

The @ character was the codepoint we wanted to replace with `()`. As we defined `insert_replaced: [0,2]`, @ was inserted as the codepoint in positions 0 and 2 of the `()` string.

See also

▶ In the *Using regular expressions* recipe, we use the `Regex` module instead of the `String` module to perform the same operations.

Slicing strings with ranges

In the *Splitting strings* recipe, we saw how to use a token (by default, a whitespace) to split a string and get a list of strings delimited by that token. What if we wish to get only a portion of the original string?

Getting ready

We will use IEx. Start it by entering `iex` in the command line.

How to do it...

To slice a string using a range, follow these steps:

1. Define a string:

   ```
   iex(1)> my_string = "The quick brown fox jumps over the lazy dog"
   "The quick brown fox jumps over the lazy dog"
   ```

2. Define two ranges:

   ```
   iex(2)> my_range_one = 10..14
   10..14
   iex(3)> my_range_two = -27..-25
   -27..-25
   ```

3. Use the `String.slice/2` function to slice the original string using `my_range_one`:

```
iex(4)> String.slice(my_string, my_range_one)
"brown"
```

4. Use the `String.slice/2` function to slice the original string using `my_range_two`:

```
iex(4)> String.slice(my_string, my_range_two)
"fox"
```

How it works...

The `String.slice/2` function uses a range to determine the start position of the split and the number of codepoints desired. As we saw in this chapter's *Introduction* section, a string is a binary that represents a succession of byte-encoded UTF-8 codepoints. To make our reasoning simpler, let's think of a string as a list, array, or vector of characters. The first codepoint will be located at position 0, and the last one will be located at position `String.length - 1`. When we pass a range, we are implicitly determining the index of the first codepoint we want and the length of the desired substring. In step 2, we started at position 10 and took five successive codepoints. The `10..14` range has five elements.

In step 3, we used a negative integer value as the range start point. This means that we wish to start counting backwards from position 27 and take three codepoints.

There's more...

The `String` module also defines the `slice/3` function, which takes as arguments a string, the starting index, and the length (`String.slice(string, start, length)`). It can be implemented as follows:

▶ To perform the slicing operation from step 3, we will write the following:

```
iex(5)> String.slice(my_string, 10, 5)
"brown"
```

▶ To perform the slicing operation from step 4, we will write the following:

```
iex(5)> String.slice(my_string, -27, 3)
"fox"
```

Using regular expressions

Elixir supports regular expressions via Erlang's `re` module. This is one of those situations that we mentioned in the *Using Erlang from Elixir* recipe in *Chapter 1, Command Line*. However, we don't have to use the `re` Erlang module directly! We have the Elixir `Regex` module that is built on top of the Erlang module and is also based on **Perl Compatible Regular Expressions** (**PCRE**).

In this recipe, we use the ~r sigil to define regular expressions and operate on strings.

 The ~r sigil is a special form that allows for the creation of regular expressions as alternatives to the Regex.compile!/2 function. Internally, a regular expression is represented by the Regex **struct** (%Regex{}).

Getting ready

Start a new IEx session by entering iex in your command line.

How to do it...

We perform the same operation we did in the *Replacing string codepoints with patterns* recipe, as follows:

1. Define a string to operate on:

   ```
   iex(1)> my_string = "user1@server.domain user2@server.domain"
   "user1@server.domain user2@server.domain"
   ```

2. Define a regular expression using the ~r sigil:

   ```
   iex(2)> my_regex = ~r{@}
   ~r/@/
   ```

3. Check whether my_string contains the defined my_regex regular expression:

   ```
   iex(3)> Regex.match?(my_regex, my_string)
   true
   ```

4. Perform the replacement of the pattern defined by the regular expression (@) in my_string with (at):

   ```
   iex(4)> Regex.replace(my_regex, my_string, "(at)")
   "user1(at)server.domain user2(at)server.domain"
   ```

5. To perform the replacement only in the first found occurrence, set the global option to false:

   ```
   iex(5)> Regex.replace(my_regex, my_string, "(at)", global: false)
   "user1(at)server.domain user2@server.domain"
   ```

6. It is also possible to reinsert the matched pattern in the replacement string:

   ```
   iex(6)> Regex.replace(my_regex, my_string, fn  -> "(#{Regex.source(my_regex)})" end)
   "user1(@)server.domain user2(@)server.domain"
   ```

How it works...

In step 1, we start by defining a string to operate upon, and in step 2, we use the ~r sigil to define the regular expression. In this case, we wish to match the @ codepoint.

> The regular expression in step 2 can also be created using the `Regex.compile!` function:
>
> `iex(2)> Regex.compile!("@")`

In step 3, we check whether the defined pattern exists in `my_string`; the return value `true` indicates that it does.

When the `Regex.replace` function is invoked without explicit options, the `global` option defaults to `true`, so all occurrences of the pattern defined in the regex are replaced. This is what happens in step 4 as opposed to step 5, where we pass `global: false`. By doing so, only the first occurrence of the pattern is replaced.

In step 6, we pass an anonymous function as an option (`fn -> "(#{Regex.source (my_regex)})" end`). Let's take a closer look at it:

- Using `fn ->` means that we don't wish to use any arguments in the anonymous function.
- The `"(#{Regex.source(my_regex)})"` part is a string interpolation (`#{}`), which means that we wish to insert the value of `Regex.source(my_regex)` inside parenthesis. The `Regex.source` function returns the pattern we defined.
- Using the anonymous function, we replace any occurrence of the pattern defined by regex with `(my_regex)`.

See also

- In the *Replacing string codepoints with patterns* recipe, we use the `String` module instead of the `Regex` module to perform the same operations.

Combining operations with the |> operator

In this recipe, we will make use of the pipe operator (`|>`) to create a series of transformations in a text file.

The `|>` operator feeds the result of the left-hand side expression as the first argument of the right-hand side expression. It is possible to create complex transformations on data, giving the programmer a more immediate perception of the data flow.

We will parse a text file, make all characters uppercase, replace every vowel with @, and save it as a new file.

Getting ready

We will create a Mix project and **escriptize** it to allow us to run it from the command line without having to start an IEx session. The steps are as follows:

1. Create a Mix project:

    ```
    > mix new pipe_transformation
    ```

2. Edit the `mix.exs` file, adding the `escript` option so that `def project` looks like this:

    ```
    def project do
        [app: :pipe_transformation,
         version: "0.0.1",
         elixir: "~> 1.0.0",
         escript: [main_module: PipeTransformation],
         deps: deps]
    end
    ```

> The `escript` option defines a main module as the entry point for the application once it is invoked from the command line.
>
> In this case, we define `PipeTransformation` as the main module, which means that it has a main function defined.

3. Add the following code to the `lib/pipe_transformation.ex` file:

    ```
    require Logger

    defmodule PipeTransformation do
      def main(args) do
        options = parse_args(args)
        Logger.info "PipeTransformation"
        Logger.info "Input file: #{options[:input]} Output
          file: #{options[:output]}"
        Logger.info "Transformation started ..."
        perform_transformation(options)
        Logger.info "Transformation finished ..."
      end

      defp parse_args(args) do
        {options, _, _} = OptionParser.parse(
                            args,
                            switches: [
                                        input: :string,
    ```

```
                                          output: :string
                                        ]
                            )
              options
            end

            defp perform_transformation(options) do
              File.stream!(options[:input]) |>
              Stream.map(&String.upcase(&1)) |>
              Stream.map(&String.replace(&1, ~r{[AEIOU]}, "@")) |>
              Stream.into(File.stream!(options[:output])) |>
              Stream.run
            end
          end
```

4.   Run the Mix task to escriptize the application:

     ```
     > mix escript.build
     ```

How to do it...

To perform our transformation, we only need to execute the application in our command line, passing the input and output files as arguments:

1.   In the `code` directory for this chapter inside the `pipe_transformation` folder, there is a file we will use as the input (`input_file.txt`).

2.   We will define the output file as `out.txt`, but you are free to name it whatever you like!

3.   Let's perform our data transformation by entering the following in the command line:

     ```
     > ./pipe_transformation --input input_file.txt --output
       out.txt
     ```

How it works...

Once the application is started via the command line, the main function in the `PipeTransformation` module is invoked. We start by parsing the command line arguments, and we invoke the private function `perform_transformation`, passing the `options` keyword list containing the input and output files. Let's take a closer look at the `perform_transformation` function:

```
defp perform_transformation(options) do
  File.stream!(options[:input]) |>
  Stream.map(&String.upcase(&1)) |>
    Stream.map(&String.replace(&1, ~r{[AEIOU]}, "@")) |>
```

```
        Stream.into(File.stream!(options[:output])) |>
        Stream.run
    end
```

We start by opening the input file as a stream, and then we perform two consecutive map operations on each element of the stream. First, we make every character uppercase, and then if the character is a vowel (uppercase), we replace it with @. Next, we define the output file and only when we invoke `Stream.run` is the whole computation performed. In the output file, you will find the result of the transformations performed on the input file.

We used the `Stream` module to show the processing in a larger string. The whole text file behaves exactly as a string.

If we wanted to perform the same transformation on a "simple" string, we can do the following:

```
iex(1)> "Lorem ipsum" |> String.upcase |> String.replace(~r{[AEIOU]},
"@")
```

```
"L@R@M @PS@M"
```

Creating a word list

In the *Using regular expressions* recipe, we used a sigil to define a regular expression. A sigil is an alternative way to define structures that have a textual representation within the language.

This recipe will show you the use of the ~W and ~w sigils to create word lists.

Getting ready

Start a new IEx session by entering `iex` in the command line.

How to do it...

To define word lists using sigils, perform the following steps:

1. Define a word list with no interpolation:

   ```
   iex(1)> ~W(one two "three" ^ @ \| 12345)
   ["one", "two", "\"three\"", "^", "@", "\\|", "12345"]
   ```

2. Define a word list with an interpolation:

   ```
   iex(2)> x = 5
   5
   iex(3)> ~w(one two #{x} five#{x} "#{x}")
   ["one", "two", "5", "five5", "\"5\""]
   ```

How it works...

When using the ~w and ~W sigils, we don't need to enclose any of the strings in "". We can even use "", and they will be escaped in the resulting list.

In step 1, we use the ~W sigil to define a word list. This sigil does not allow string interpolation. In step 2, we define the word list with ~w. This sigil allows string interpolation. We used string interpolation to include the value of x in the generated word list.

There's more...

Sigils can be defined using ~, followed by the sigil symbol (W, w, r, and so on) and the text inside delimiters.

 The delimiters used with sigils can be any of these: \ \, | |, ( ), " ", ' ', [ ], { }, and < >.

Determining the word frequency in a text

In this recipe, we will load a text file, extract the words from it, and then determine the number of times each of these words appears in the text.

The output will be written into a new file named word_frequency.txt, where the words found in the text will be sorted and followed by an integer indicating their frequency in the text.

Getting ready

We will create a new Mix project and **escriptize** it, allowing us to run it as a command-line application:

1. Create a new Mix project:

   ```
   > mix new word_frequency
   ```

2. Add the escript option to the mix.exs file, indicating where the main function is located; in this case, it will be in the WordFrequency module:

   ```
   def project do
     [app: :word_frequency,
     version: "0.0.1",
     elixir: "~> 1.0.0",
     escript: [main_module: WordFrequency],
     deps: deps]
   end
   ```

How to do it...

We will be adding all the required code to the `lib/word_frequency.ex` file. Open it in your editor and let's get started:

1. We will be using the `Logger` module to output information, so start by requiring the module on the first line of the source file:

```
require Logger
```

2. Next, define our `main` function:

```
def main(args) do
  options = parse_args(args)
  Logger.info "Input file: #{options[:file]}"
  word_frequency_map = File.stream!(options[:file]) |>
                          get_word_list_stream |>
                          count_words
  Logger.info "Processing entries ..."
  write_to_file(word_frequency_map)
  Logger.info "File word_frequency.txt written !"
end
```

3. Define a private function to parse the command-line arguments:

```
defp parse_args(args) do
  {options, _, _} = OptionParser.parse(
                      args, switches: [file: :string]
                    )
  options
end
```

4. The next (private) function we need to define is `get_word_list_stream`:

```
defp get_word_list_stream(file_stream) do
  map_fn = fn x -> String.split(x, ~r{[^A-Za-z0-9_]}) end
  filter_fn = fn x -> String.length(x) > 0 end
  file_stream |>
  Stream.flat_map(map_fn) |>
  Stream.filter(filter_fn)
end
```

5. Now, define the `count_words` function(s):

```
defp count_words(stream) do
  count_words(Enum.to_list(stream),Map.new)
end
defp count_words([], map), do: map
defp count_words([word|rest], map) do
```

```
      case Map.has_key?(map, word) do
        true ->
          map = Map.update!(map, word, fn(val) -> val + 1 end)
          count_words(rest, map)
        false ->
          map = Map.put_new(map, word, 1)
          count_words(rest, map)
      end
    end
```

6. The last function we need to define is `write_to_file`:

```
defp write_to_file(map) do
  reduce = fn(key, acc) ->
             acc <> "#{key}: #{Map.get(map, key)} time(s)\n"
           end
  output = map |> Map.keys |> Enum.reduce(" ", reduce)
  File.write!("word_frequency.txt", output)
end
```

7. Let's make our project executable from the command line by running the `escript.build` Mix task:

```
> mix escript.build
Consolidated Access
Consolidated Collectable
Consolidated Enumerable
Consolidated Inspect
Consolidated List.Chars
Consolidated Range.Iterator
Consolidated String.Chars
Consolidated protocols written to _build/dev/consolidated
```

8. Now, it's time to run our application:

```
> ./word_frequency --file walt_whitman.txt
17:56:45.795 [info]  Input file: walt_whitman.txt
17:56:45.824 [info]  Processing entries ...
17:56:45.827 [info]  File word_frequency.txt written !
```

9. The `word_frequency.txt` file was written to the disk and inside it, you will find the words from the input file and see how many times they appear:

```
● ○ ○                          word_frequency.txt
push: 1 time(s)
ribboned: 1 time(s)
ring: 1 time(s)
rise: 1 time(s)
safe: 1 time(s)
ship: 4 time(s)
shores: 2 time(s)
silent: 1 time(s)
some: 1 time(s)
sought: 1 time(s)
spot: 2 time(s)
steady: 1 time(s)
still: 1 time(s)
swaying: 1 time(s)
that: 1 time(s)
the: 17 time(s)
their: 1 time(s)
they: 1 time(s)
tread: 1 time(s)
trills: 1 time(s)
trip: 2 time(s)
turning: 1 time(s)
up: 2 time(s)
ye: 1 time(s)
vessel: 1 time(s)
victor: 1 time(s)
voyage: 1 time(s)
we: 1 time(s)
weathered: 1 time(s)
will: 1 time(s)
```

How it works...

In this recipe, we created a small command-line application to determine the word frequency in the text stored in a file. The file we use (`walt_whitman.txt`) was taken from the Project Gutenberg website (`http://www.gutenberg.org`) and can be found in the source code under the `word_frequency` folder.

We start by requiring the `Logger` module in step 1. This allows us to use `Logger.info` to output information on our running application.

In step 2, we define the `main` function. This is necessary because we want to run this application as a command-line tool by "escriptizing" it. The `main` function has a series of sequential instructions that represent our application flow. You will find them as highlighted code. We will see each operation in detail in the explanation of next steps, but to give you a general idea, we can simplify the flow as follows:

1. Parse the command-line arguments.

2. Read the file, clean it up, and process each word.

3. Write the result to a file.

We begin by parsing the command-line arguments. In step 3, we use the `OptionParse.parse` function to get the `--file` option as a string.

This string indicates the path of the input file where the text to be processed is stored.

We use the file path to load it as a stream, and we pass this stream to the `get_word_list_stream` function defined in step 4. The function has two anonymous functions defined, which will be used to map and filter the file stream we get as the input:

- `map_fn = fn x -> String.split(x, ~r{[^A-Za-z0-9_]})  end`: This function uses a regular expression to split the input strings, removing all nonwords.

- `filter_fn = fn x -> String.length(x) > 0 end`: This function selects all strings with the nonzero length.

In the last line of the `get_word_list_stream` function, we perform a series of transformations to the input file stream, and we also get a stream as result. If you recall the *Generating lazy (even infinite) sequences* recipe in *Chapter 2, Data Types and Structures*, when we use streams, no intermediary values are used, which means that no computation has been performed effectively.

Let's take a look at the transformation:

```
file_stream |>
Stream.flat_map(map_fn) |>
Stream.filter(filter_fn)
```

We start by feeding the file stream into the `flat_map` function that returns a flattened list (actually, it's not yet a list as a stream performs lazy evaluation; think of it as the plan to get a list) of strings. If we used just the map function, we would get a list of lists as the file is read line by line and each line would result in a list of strings. The `flat_map` function transforms a list of lists into a simple list. This resulting list is then filtered and all the strings with the 0 length are removed (whitespaces).

The function defined in step 4 returns a stream that we will use as an input to the `count_words` function defined in the next step.

In step 5, we define a recursive function named `count_words`. Pattern matching is used to determine which form of the function is used. We have three possibilities:

- `count_words(stream)`: This function is matched when the input is a stream—actually, when the input is a single argument!

  In this function, we receive the stream and transform it into a list; we create an empty map and we start the recursion.

- `count_words([], map) , do: map`: This function is matched when an empty list is passed and it actually returns the map received as the input! This is where we stop the recursion.

- `count_words([word|rest], map)`: This function is matched every time we pass a nonempty list and map to `count_words`.

We then perform a match (case) by checking whether the map contains the word as a key. If it does, we increment the value by one, and if it doesn't, we create a new entry in the map with the word as the key and 1 as its value. We then pass the rest of the list and the resulting map to continue the recursion.

In step 6, we define the `write_to_file` function to format data and write it into the output file.

We start by defining a `reduce` anonymous function:

```
reduce = fn(key, acc) -> acc <> "#{key}: #{Map.get(map, key)}
time(s)\n" end
```

In `reduce`, we receive a key and an accumulator, and then we concatenate the key and its value that we get from the map to the accumulator.

This anonymous `reduce` function is used in the `output = map |> Map.keys |> Enum.reduce("", reduce)` transformation.

We start by passing the map to `Map.keys`, which returns a list of the keys present in the map, and we feed that list into `Enum.reduce`. The accumulator will start as an empty string and all keys and values will then be concatenated.

The last step is to write the result of this transformation to the output file.

In step 7, we run the `escript.build` Mix task, which will transform our project in a command-line executable.

To run the application, pass the `--file <filename>` option, and the result will be saved in the application directory as the `word_frequency.txt` file.

Reading and writing metadata from MP3 files

In this chapter's introduction, we mentioned the fact that in Elixir, strings are binaries. In this recipe, we will use a binary file (an MP3 file) and apply some of the operations that we previously performed on strings. We will pattern match the MP3 binary file to extract some information—ID3 v2 information—and we will replace a portion of the file—ID3 v1 information—by constructing a new string and concatenating it to the end of the binary file. In the end, we will still have a proper MP3 file that we will be able to play on our favorite music player!

 MP3 files have some metadata stored on them in the form of ID3 tags. The first version of the ID3 tag was stored in the last 128 bytes of the file. The new ID3 tag (v2) is stored at the beginning of the file and may have variable length.

Getting ready

To get started, create a new `mp3_info.ex` file and add the following code:

```elixir
defmodule Mp3Info do

  @file_name "Divider.mp3"

  def id3_v2_basic_info(input_file \\ @file_name) do
    {:ok, mp3_file} = File.read(input_file)
    <<  tag_id    :: binary-size(3),
        major_v   :: unsigned-integer-size(8),
        revision  :: unsigned-integer-size(8),
        _         :: bitstring >> = mp3_file
    IO.puts """
    [ID3v2 Info]
    Tag:            #{tag_id}
    Major Version:  #{major_v}
    Revision:       #{revision}
    """
  end

  def id3_v1_info(input_file \\ @file_name) do
    {:ok, mp3_file} = File.read(input_file)
    mp3_size_without_id3 = (byte_size(mp3_file) - 128)
    << _ :: binary-size(mp3_size_without_id3), id3_v1_tag_data ::
binary >> = mp3_file

    << tag      :: binary-size(3),
       title    :: binary-size(30),
       artist   :: binary-size(30),
       album    :: binary-size(30),
       year     :: binary-size(4),
       comments :: binary-size(30),
       _        :: binary >> = id3_v1_tag_data

    IO.puts """
    [ID3v1 Info]
    Tag:            #{tag}
    Title:          #{title}
    Artist:         #{artist}
    Album:          #{album}
    Year:           #{year}
```

```
    Comments:           #{comments}
    """
  end


  def write_info(input_file \\ @file_name, output_file \\ "new.mp3")
do
    {:ok, mp3_file} = File.read(input_file)
    tag        = "TAG"
    author     = pad("Chris Zabriskie", 30)
    title      = pad("Divider", 30)
    album      = pad("Divider", 30)
    year       = "2011"
    comments = pad("Copyright: Creative Commons", 30)

    tag_to_write = pad((tag <> author <> title <> album <> year <>
comments), 128)

    mp3_size_without_id3 = (byte_size(mp3_file) - 128)
    << other_data :: binary-size(mp3_size_without_id3), _ :: binary >>
= mp3_file

    File.write(output_file, (other_data <> tag_to_write))
  end


  defp pad(string, desired_size) do
    String.ljust(string,desired_size)
  end

end
```

We are hardcoding some information to be placed in the ID3v1 tag of the mp3 file. So if you are able to, download the Divider.mp3 file bundled with the code and place it in the same directory as the mp3_info.ex file.

How to do it...

To read and write ID3 information to a binary (MP3) file, follow these steps:

1. Start IEx, loading the mp3_info.ex file:

   > **iex mp3_info.ex**

2. Read the version from the ID3 v2 tag in the MP3 file:

```
iex(1)> Mp3Info.id3_v2_basic_info
[ID3v2 Info]
Tag:              ID3
Major Version:    4
Revision:         0

:ok
```

3. Read the current ID3 v1 metadata from the MP3 file:

```
iex(2)> Mp3Info.id3_v1_info
[ID3v1 Info]
Tag:         UUU
Title:       UUUUUUUUUUUUUUUUUUUUUUUUUUUUUUUUU
Artist:      UUUUUUUUUUUUUUUUUUUUUUUUUUUUUUUUU
Album:       UUUUUUUUUUUUUUUUUUUUUUUUUUUUUUUUU
Year:        UUUU
Comments:    UUUUUUUUUUUUUUUUUUUUUUUUUUUUUUUUU

:ok
```

4. As the information we got in the last step is no good, let's replace it:

```
iex(3)> Mp3Info.write_info
:ok
```

 In this step, a new file is created. By default, if no arguments are passed onto the `write_info` function, it will read the `Divider.mp3` file and output to the `new.mp3` file.

5. Check whether the ID3 v1 information was correctly written on the file:

```
iex(4)> Mp3Info.id3_v1_info "new.mp3"
[ID3v1 Info]
Tag:         TAG
Title:       Chris Zabriskie
Artist:      Divider
Album:       Divider
Year:        2011
Comments:    Copyright: Creative Commons

:ok
```

6. Finally, the most important step when we talk about MP3 files is to open the `new.mp3` file on your favorite music player and enjoy it!

How it works...

The module we created contains functions to read ID3 v1 tags and the version of ID3 v2 tags, as well as a function that replaces the last 128 bytes of an MP3 file with new data, and then joins it to a new file.

In step 2, we begin by getting the version of the ID3 v2 tag used in the MP3 file.

To do this, we begin by reading the binary file, assigning it to `mp3_file`:

```
{:ok, mp3_file} = File.read(input_file)
```

We then pattern match the file to extract the first five bytes containing the information we need. The first three bytes contain the `ID3` string, and the next two bytes are integers representing the `major_version` value of the tag and the revision:

```
<<  tag_id    :: binary-size(3),
    major_v   :: unsigned-integer-size(8),
    revision  :: unsigned-integer-size(8),
    _         :: bitstring >> = mp3_file
```

In the preceding code, we use the following pattern:

```
<< variable1 :: <type>-size(<size in bits or bytes>),
variable2 :: <type>-size(<size in bits or bytes>),
variable n :: <type>-size(<size in bits or bytes>) >> =
binary_to_match
```

The last entry in our pattern match is `_ :: bitstring`. If you recall pattern matching, this means that we don't care about that variable. We are actually extracting the first five bytes and stating that we don't care about the remainder of the file. To recap, `tag_id` is a binary (string) represented by three bytes, so we read it using `binary-size(3)`. Binary sizes are "measured" in bytes. Then we read `major_v`, saying we wish to retrieve it as an unsigned integer with the size of 8 bits (1 byte). We do the same for `revision`.

As the major version is 4 and the revision is 0, this means that this is an ID3 v2.4.0 tag.

In step 3, we read the information contained in the ID3 v1 section of the file. The ID3 v1 tag is contained within the last 128 bytes of the file.

As with the previous step, we start by reading the binary file and assigning it to the `mp3_file`. We then determine the file size, excluding the last 128 bytes:

```
mp3_size_without_id3 = (byte_size(mp3_file) - 128)
```

Then we pattern match on `mp3_file`:

```
<< _               :: binary-size(mp3_size_without_id3),
   id3_v1_tag_data :: binary >> = mp3_file
```

We start by declaring that we don't care about the starting bytes of the file by assigning all of the bytes other than the last 128 to _ and assigning the last 128 bytes of the file to id3_v1_tag_data.

We then pattern match again on `id3_v1_tag_data` to deconstruct it in its components.

You can find more information about the layout of an ID3 v1 tag at `http://en.wikipedia. org/wiki/ID3#Layout`.

To briefly sum it up, we read three bytes for the tag, 30 bytes for the title, 30 bytes for the artist, 30 bytes for the album, 30 bytes for the year, 30 bytes for the comments, and we discard the remaining bytes:

```
<< tag       :: binary-size(3),
   title     :: binary-size(30),
   artist    :: binary-size(30),
   album     :: binary-size(30),
   year      :: binary-size(4),
   comments  :: binary-size(30),
   _         :: binary >> = id3_v1_tag_data
```

In step 3, we create a new string with the information we desire to insert on the MP3 file:

```
tag_to_write = pad((tag <> author <> title <> album <> year <>
comments), 128)
```

We use the `<>` operator to concatenate the strings, and the `pad` function ensures that the strings have a given amount of bytes. We need to do this to make sure each string fits the correct place in the ID3 v1 structure:

```
defp pad(string, desired_size) do
  String.ljust(string, desired_size)
end
```

Afterwards, we get the original file content without the last 128 bytes:

```
mp3_size_without_id3 = (byte_size(mp3_file) - 128)
<< other_data :: binary-size(mp3_size_without_id3), _ :: binary >>
  = mp3_file
```

We concatenate it with our new tag, writing to a new file:

```
File.write(output_file, (other_data <> tag_to_write))
```

There's more...

Erlang, given its telecom origins, has amazing support for mapping protocols via binaries. In this recipe, we used an MP3 file, but we could have easily used an IP packet and using the same techniques, we could have deconstructed it. All we need to know is the protocol format, and then mapping to a data structure is an easy task!

This recipe was heavily inspired by the following blog posts: `https://taizilla.wordpress.com/2009/09/14/erl_id3v2/` and `http://benjamintan.io/blog/2014/06/10/elixir-bit-syntax-and-id3/`.

4
Modules and Functions

This chapter will cover the following recipes:

- ▶ Namespacing modules
- ▶ Using module attributes as constants
- ▶ Enforcing behaviors
- ▶ Documenting modules
- ▶ Using module directives
- ▶ Using a module in the scripted mode
- ▶ Defining functions with default arguments
- ▶ Using guard clauses and pattern matching in function definitions

Introduction

Elixir modules are files (see the following information box) where related functions are grouped and stored. In *Chapter 1, Command Line*, we covered how to load and compile our own modules in IEx and how to generate applications with Mix. Mix applications are a collection of modules within a predefined directory structure.

Modules are defined using the `defmodule` macro and functions using the `def` and `defp` macros.

In this chapter, we will be developing some concepts that are specifically related to modules and functions. It is also possible to define modules inside IEx without storing them to files.

Namespacing modules

We can think of a module as a namespace. Every function defined inside a module has to be prepended with that module's name in order to be invoked elsewhere.

It is also possible to store our modules inside directories in order to better organize them to suit our purpose or intent.

In this recipe, we will show you how to namespace modules and use them.

Getting ready

In this recipe, we will use a Mix application. You will find the application in the source code folder under `chapter3/demo`. Navigate to the application directory in your terminal window and compile the project to make sure everything is ready:

```
> cd Code/Chapter 4/demo
> mix compile
```

How to do it...

In order to demonstrate the use of three namespaced modules within our generated Mix application, follow these steps:

1. Modify the `lib/demo.ex` file by adding the `run_me` function:

   ```
   def run_me(name \\ "Stranger") do
     IO.puts " #{__MODULE__} says \"Hi there #{name}!\""
     Demo.Greeter.greet
     Demo.One.Greeter.greet
     Demo.Two.Greeter.greet
   end
   ```

2. Start a new IEx session and load the project:

   ```
   > iex -S mix
   ```

3. Invoke the `run_me` function defined in step 1:

   ```
   iex(1)> Demo.run_me
   Elixir.Demo says "Hi there Stranger!"
   Elixir.Demo.Greeter says "Hi there!"
   Elixir.Demo.One.Greeter says "Hello!"
   Elixir.Demo.Two.Greeter says "Howdy!"
   :ok
   ```

How it works...

The demo project contains the Demo, Demo.Greeter, Demo.One.Greeter, and Demo.Two.Greeter modules:

```
Module              File            Location
Demo                demo.ex         lib/demo.ex
Demo.Greeter        greeter.ex      lib/demo/greeter.ex
Demo.One.Greeter    greeter.ex      lib/demo/one/greeter.ex
Demo.Two.Greeter    greeter.ex      lib/demo/two/greeter.ex
```

The run_me function we created in step 1 calls the greet function defined in each of the namespaced modules. These modules are all defined in a file with the same name (greeter.ex), but the folder structure allows us to organize our modules in different namespaces.

There's more...

If you take a look at the _build/dev/lib/demo/ebin folder, where our compiled code is, you will see that all Elixir modules are defined inside the Elixir namespace and they are actually stored in the same directory.

Using module attributes as constants

Elixir supports the definition of module attributes using the @ syntax. There are a few reserved module attributes: @moduledoc, @doc, @behaviour, and @before_compile. We will focus on some of them in the next two recipes.

In this recipe, we will use module attributes as constants and access them inside functions.

 Module attributes can only be defined outside functions and can be defined more than once in a module.

How to do it...

To use module attributes as constants, follow these steps:

1. Create a new constants.ex module and add the following code:

```
defmodule Constants do
  @name "Bill"
  @age 22

  def function_one do
```

```
      IO.puts("#{@name} is #{@age} years old.")
    end

    @name "Joe"
    def function_two do
      IO.puts("#{@name} is #{@age+1} years old.")
    end
  end
```

2. Start an IEx session in the same directory where you saved `constants.ex`:

    ```
    > iex constants.ex
    ```

     Instead of starting IEx and then loading and compiling the module, it is possible to indicate the name of the module as an argument to the `iex` command.

3. Invoke `function_one`:

    ```
    iex(2)> Constants.function_one
    Bill is 22 years old.
    :ok
    ```

4. Invoke `function_two`:

    ```
    iex(3)> Constants.function_two
    Joe is 23 years old.
    :ok
    ```

How it works...

In the `Constants` module, we defined the `@name` and `@age` module attributes.

In step 3, we use both of these module attributes in `function_one`, interpolating them in a string.

In step 4, we get a different value for `@name` because the module attribute is redefined immediately before the `function_two` definition. The `@age` attribute is the same (22), but we added 1 to it in the string interpolation (`#{@age+1}`).

See also

▶   In the *Managing application configuration* recipe in *Chapter 1, Command Line*, we already used module attributes.

▶   The *Enforcing behaviors* and *Documenting modules* recipes in this chapter also use (reserved) module attributes.

Enforcing behaviors

One of the reserved module attributes in Elixir is `@behaviour`. It is used to ensure that a given module implements the required callbacks and that the module implements a given interface and behaves in a defined way.

How to do it...

To demonstrate the use of the `@behaviour` module attribute, follow these steps:

1. Create the `Randomizer` module inside the `randomizer.ex` file by adding the following code:

```
defmodule Randomizer do
  use Behaviour
  defcallback randomize(low::Integer.t, high::Integer.t) ::
    Integer.t
end
```

2. Create a module to implement the `Randomizer` behavior inside the `my_module.ex` file by adding the following code:

```
defmodule MyModule do
  @behaviour Randomizer
end
```

3. Open a new IEx session in the same directory where the modules defined in steps 1 and 2 are stored:

```
> iex
```

4. Compile both modules starting with `Randomizer`:

```
iex(1)> c("randomizer.ex")
[Randomizer]
iex(2)> c("my_module.ex")
my_module.ex:1: warning: undefined behaviour function randomize/2
(for behaviour Randomizer)
[MyModule]
```

5. To address the `undefined behaviour` warning from the previous step, add the following code to `my_module.ex`:

```
def randomize(low, high) when low < high do
  :crypto.rand_uniform(low, high)
end
```

6. Recompile `MyModule`:

```
iex(3)> c("my_module.ex")
my_module.ex:1: warning: redefining module MyModule
[MyModule]
```

How it works...

In step 1, we created the `Randomizer` module and defined a callback via the `defcallback` macro:

```
defcallback randomize(low::Integer.t, high::Integer.t) :: Integer.t
```

In the `randomize` callback, we defined the `low` and `high` arguments as the `Integer` type, and we also stated that the return type would also be an integer. You can think of it as a contract that any module has to conform to in order to implement the `Randomizer` behavior.

In step 2, we created `MyModule` and annotated it with the reserved `@behaviour` module attribute.

When we compiled `MyModule` (in step 4), we got a warning as `undefined behaviour function randomize/2 (for behaviour Randomizer)`. This warning means that `MyModule` doesn't implement the `randomize/2` function we defined as a callback in the `Randomizer` module.

In step 5, we implemented `randomize/2` in `MyModule`, and in step 6, we recompile it, and the warning about undefined behavior is gone!

See also

> ▸ The `MyModule.randomize` function uses a guard (when `low` is less than `high`). To learn more about guards, check the *Using guard clauses and pattern matching in functions* recipe.

Documenting modules

In this recipe, we will be using the `@moduledoc` and `@doc` reserved module attributes to add documentation to the modules we defined in the previous recipe, *Enforcing behaviors*.

Getting ready

Open the `randomizer.ex` and `my_module.ex` files created in the *Enforcing behaviors* recipe inside your preferred code editor.

How to do it...

To add documentation to our modules, follow these steps:

1. We will start by adding module documentation to the `randomizer.ex` file. Add the following code below the `use Behavior` line:

```
@moduledoc """
  This module specifies the interface for a randomizer behaviour
by using the defcallback macro.
"""
```

2. Add the following module documentation to the `my_module.ex` file below the `@ behaviour Randomizer` line:

```
@moduledoc """
  This is a custom module to demo the implementation of
behaviours.
"""
```

3. To document the `randomize` function inside `my_module.ex`, insert the following code right above the function definition:

```
@doc """
The randomize callback defines the randomize function taking 2
arguments:
    low:  an Integer with the lower boundary
    thigh: an Integer with the upper boundary
The function outputs an Integer. The output is comprised within
the [low;high] interval. This function uses a guard to ensure it
is only invoked when low value is smaller than high value.
This function uses the rand_uniform function from erlang's crypto
module(http://www.erlang.org/doc/man/crypto.html).
"""
```

4. To see the result of our documentation work, open a new IEx session in the same directory where `randomizer.ex` and `my_module.ex` are present and load/compile both files:

```
> iex

iex(1)> c("randomizer.ex")

[Randomizer]

iex(2)> c("my_module.ex")

[MyModule]
```

5. To get information about the modules and the `randomize` function, we will use the h command inside IEx, as we saw in the *Getting help and accessing documentation within IEx* recipe in *Chapter 1, Command Line*, and access documentation within IEx. The following screenshot shows you the result:

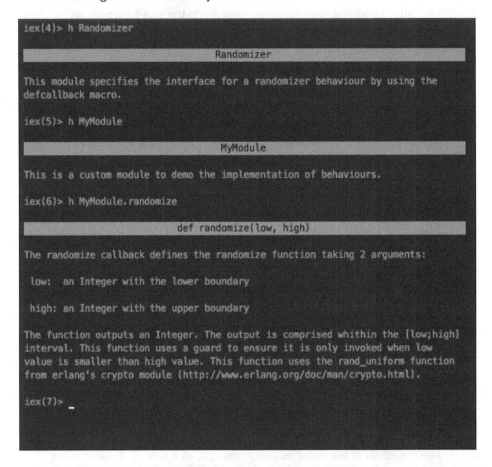

```
iex(4)> h Randomizer

                          Randomizer

This module specifies the interface for a randomizer behaviour by using the
defcallback macro.

iex(5)> h MyModule

                           MyModule

This is a custom module to demo the implementation of behaviours.

iex(6)> h MyModule.randomize

                     def randomize(low, high)

The randomize callback defines the randomize function taking 2 arguments:

  low:  an Integer with the lower boundary

  high: an Integer with the upper boundary

The function outputs an Integer. The output is comprised whithin the [low;high]
interval. This function uses a guard to ensure it is only invoked when low
value is smaller than high value. This function uses the rand_uniform function
from erlang's crypto module (http://www.erlang.org/doc/man/crypto.html).

iex(7)> _
```

Using module directives

To simplify working with modules, Elixir provides three directives: `import`, `alias`, and `require`. These three module directives are lexically scoped—if defined in the module scope, they are valid for the whole module, but if defined inside a function, they are only valid inside that function.

These three directives allow the use of code defined in other modules.

Getting ready

Create the `require_me.ex` file with the following content:

```
defmodule RequireMe do
  def foo do
    IO.puts "This is foo from #{__MODULE__} module"
  end
end
```

In the same folder, create the `directives.ex` file and add the following code:

```
defmodule Directives do
  @col   [1,2,3]
  @name "demo"

  # require directive

  # alias directive module scope
  alias String, as: S
  # import directive module scope
  import List, only: [first: 1]

  def test_module_alias do
    IO.puts "Name is #{S.capitalize(@name)}"
  end

  def test_function_alias do
    # alias directive function scope
    alias RequireMe, as: RM
    RM.foo
  end

  def test_module_import do
    IO.puts "First element of #{inspect(@col)} is #{first(@col)}"
  end

  def test_function_import do
    # import directive function scope
    import Enum, only: [count: 1]
    IO.puts "#{inspect(@col)} has #{count(@col)} elements"
  end
end
```

Load the `directives.ex` file in your code editor and start a new IEx session:

```
> iex directives.ex
```

How to do it...

We will see the three directives in action. We will start with `require`, and then we will look into `alias` and finally, into `import`. Let's get started!

To see the `require` directive in action, follow these steps:

1. Add the following code to `directives.ex` right below the `# require directive` comment:

    ```
    require RequireMe
    ```

2. Compile the `Directives` module inside the IEx session:

    ```
    iex(1)> c("directives.ex")
    == Compilation error on file directives.ex ==
    ** (CompileError) directives.ex:6: module RequireMe is not loaded
    and could not be found
    ```

3. Fix this error by compiling the `RequireMe` module:

    ```
    iex(1)> c("require_me.ex")
    [RequireMe]
    ```

4. Now, try again to compile the `Directives` module:

    ```
    iex(2)> c("directives.ex")
    [Directives]
    ```

To illustrate the use of the `alias` directive, we will invoke the `test_module_alias` and `test_function_alias` functions:

```
iex(3)> Directives.test_module_alias
Name is Demo
:ok
iex(4)> Directives.test_function_alias
This is foo from Elixir.RequireMe module
:ok
```

Finally, let's see the use of the `import` directive by invoking the `test_module_import` and `test_function_import` functions:

```
iex(5)> Directives.test_module_import
```

```
First element of [1, 2, 3] is 1
:ok
iex(6)> Directives.test_function_import
[1, 2, 3] has 3 elements
:ok
```

How it works...

In step 2, we got a compilation error when we tried to compile the `Directives` module. This happened because we required the `RequireMe` module while the module was not yet compiled and loaded, so it wasn't available for inclusion. The `require` directive ensures that the required module has to be loaded before any code tries to use it. By compiling and loading the `RequireMe` module in step 3, we are finally able to compile the `Directives` module.

The `alias` directive allows us to simplify code; in the `Directives` module, we use it to shorten `String` to `S` and `RequireMe` to `RM`.

It is also possible to use a particular function from a module without having to prepend it with the module name. The `import` directive is used in this case and in the `Directives` module, we use it to import the `List.first/1` and `Enum.count/1` functions. They become the `first` and `count` variables, and we use them in `test_module_import` and `test_function_import`.

 Note that importing a module automatically requires that module

There's more...

The `import` directive also accepts the `except` option. In the `Directives` module, we use the `only` option. With `only`, you have to specify all the functions *you wish to import*. With `except`, you have to enumerate all the functions *you don't wish to import*.

Using a module in the scripted mode

It is possible to use Elixir as if it were an interpreted language. Code is evaluated at the source level, eliminating the need to compile it before use. One of the examples of the usage of Elixir in the scripted mode is the test suite inside a Mix project. There, under the `tests` directory, you will find files with the `.exs` extension.

The convention in Elixir is to use the `.ex` extension in files that should be compiled and the `.exs` extension in files that should be interpreted.

How to do it...

To use the Elixir code without compiling it, follow these steps:

1. Create a file named `my_script.exs` and add the following code:

    ```
    %{:date => d, :version => v} = System.build_info
    IO.puts """
    Command line arguments passed: #{inspect(System.argv)}
    Elixir version: #{v} (#{d})
    """
    ```

2. Run the code in your terminal window:

    ```
    > elixir my_script.exs --demo -T -v
    Command line arguments passed: ["--demo", "-T", "-v"]
    Elixir version: 1.0.0 (Wed, 10 Sep 2014 17:30:06 GMT)
    ```

How it works...

We have created a file with code that uses pattern matching and string interpolation and invokes the `System` module. We have not defined any module or function; we have just defined a sequence of instructions we wish to carry out.

The sequence of instructions was executed using the `elixir` command-line executable.

If we take a closer look, we'll see that no `.beam` file was created and no code was compiled. The file was interpreted line-by-line.

There's more...

IEx allows the insertion of code line-by-line, and it is also possible to define modules and functions inside IEx. All of the code in IEx is interpreted, and compilation only happens when the `c("<filepath>")` function is invoked.

Defining functions with default arguments

In Elixir, named functions (defined with the `def` macro) can accept arguments and sometimes, it is convenient to assume them as optional by defining a default value or expression. Default values for function arguments are defined using \\ after the argument name.

If we define a foo(a, b, c \\ 0) function and c has a default value, although the function can be invoked as foo(1,3) with arity 2, the function foo/3 is executed, in this case, as foo(1,3,0). We don't explicitly pass a value for c but it will take the defined value, in this case, 0.

Getting ready

Load the Defaults file module inside IEx and open the file defining the module (defaults.ex) inside your favorite code editor:

```
> iex defaults.ex

[Defaults]
```

How to do it...

To define functions with default arguments, follow these steps:

1. Define a sum function in the Defaults module by adding the following code to defaults.ex:

   ```
   def sum(a, b \\ 1, c \\ 1) do
      a + b + c
   end
   ```

2. Save the file and reload it in IEx:

   ```
   iex(2)> r Defaults

   warning: redefining module Directives

   {:reloaded, Directives, [Directives]}
   ```

3. To see the default arguments in action, invoke our sum function a few times:

   ```
   iex(3)> Defaults.sum(2)

   4

   iex(4)> Defaults.sum(2,3)

   6

   iex(5)> Defaults.sum(2,3,4)

   9

   iex(6)> Defaults.sum()

   ** (UndefinedFunctionError) undefined function: Defaults.sum/0

        Defaults.sum()
   ```

How it works...

When we define default values for arguments in a function (although we might invoke the function omitting some of the optional arguments), it doesn't mean that only the passed argument will be taken into account. In step 1, the `sum` function has no default value for a and assumes a default value of 1 for b and c. This means that we can invoke `sum` by passing only one argument. The first invocation in step 3, `Defaults.sum(2)`, is equivalent to `Defaults.sum(2,1,1)`. The next time we use the `sum` function, we pass the 2 value to a and 3 to b. This means that we don't want to use the default value for b. When we call `Defaults.sum(2,3,4)`, it bypasses all default values. The final time we use `sum` in step 3, we do it without `Defaults.sum()` arguments and it fails because there's no default value for a.

Using guard clauses and pattern matching in function definitions

In the *Using pattern matching* recipe in *Chapter 2, Data Types and Structures*, we saw how it was possible to use the = operator to match values on the right-hand side with values on the left-hand side. In this recipe, we will see pattern matching in action without using the = operator. We will use pattern matching implicitly in function definitions with the same name and arity, and Elixir will use it to determine which function version to execute.

Sometimes, pattern matching is not enough to determine which function to execute, so we will also be using guard clauses in our function definitions. Guard clauses allow us to only execute a given function if some condition regarding its argument types or values is verified.

Getting ready

This is how we get started:

1. Define a new module named `PatternsAndGuards` in a file named `patterns_and_guards.ex` by inserting the following code:

   ```
   defmodule PatternsAndGuards do
     #guards
     #pattern matching
   end
   ```

2. Save the file and load it in a new IEx session:

   ```
   > iex
   iex(1)> c("patterns_and_guards.ex")
   [PatternsAndGuards]
   ```

3. Define an alias for the `PatternsAndGuards` module to reduce the typing required to invoke its functions:

```
iex(2)> alias PatternsAndGuards, as: PG
nil
```

 We saw the use of the `alias` module directive in the *Using module directives* recipe, and this seems a good time to make use of it, as it is also possible to use it inside IEx.

How to do it...

We will start by adding a print function that will have three different bodies: one to use when the input is a list, one to use when it is a string (binary), and another for every other case.

Afterwards, we will define a recursive function to print each element of a list that will pattern match the argument to determine which function definition should be executed.

Let's get started:

1. Open the `patterns_and_guards.ex` file inside your code editor.

2. Define a `print` function to print lists by adding the following code below the `#guards` comment:

```
def print(x) when is_list(x) do
    IO.puts "Printing a list -> #{inspect(x)}"
end
```

3. Define a `print` function to print binaries (a string is a binary) by adding the following code *after* the one defined in the previous step:

```
def print(x) when is_binary(x) do
    IO.puts "Printing a binary -> #{inspect(x)}"
end
```

4. Add the `print` function to handle every other type of input. This should also be inserted *below* the other print function definitions:

```
def print(x) do
    IO.puts "Printing a non-list/binary -> #{inspect(x)}"
end
```

5. Define a recursive function to print each element of a list by inserting the following code after the `#pattern matching` comment:

```
def print_each_from_list([]) do
   :ok
end
```

```
def print_each_from_list([h|t]) do
  print(h)
  print_each_from_list(t)
end
```

6. Save the file and reload it in IEx:

   iex(3)> c("patterns_and_guards.ex")

   patterns_and_guards.ex:1: warning: redefining module PatternsAndGuards

   [PatternsAndGuards]

7. Use the print function with a list:

   iex(4)> PG.print([1,2,3,4])

   Printing a list -> [1, 2, 3, 4]

   :ok

8. Now, use the print function with a string:

   iex(5)> PG.print("Demo")

   Printing a binary -> "Demo"

   :ok

9. Finally, use the print function with an atom:

   iex(6)> PG.print(:atom)

   Printing a non-list/binary -> :atom

   :ok

10. It's time to check our recursive list element printing function:

    iex(7)> PG.print_each_from_list([[1], 2, :a, "b", [5]])

    Printing a list -> [1]

    Printing a non-list/binary -> 2

    Printing a non-list/binary -> :a

    Printing a binary -> "b"

    Printing a list -> [5]

    :ok

How it works...

We will start by looking into guard clauses. Our `print` function has three different clauses:

- `def print(x) when is_list(x) do (...)`
- `def print(x) when is_binary(x) do (...)`
- `def print(x) do (...)`

The guard clause is defined using the `when` keyword, and the order of the function definitions matters. The first one that matches will be executed.

> If we reversed the order and placed `def print(x) do` first, none of the other function definitions would ever be reached as `print(x)` would always match!

The `is_list` and `is_binary` functions are used to determine the type of the argument. Based on these conditions, Elixir decides which function definition to execute, and if none of the previous conditions are met, the *general case* `print(x)` function definition is used.

Guard clauses can also take argument values into account and not just argument types. We have already used guard clauses in the *Enforcing behaviors* recipe. In the `MyModule` module, we defined a `randomize` function:

```
def randomize(low, high) when low < high do (...)
```

The guard clause in here (`low < high`) ensures that the function body will only be executed when the given condition is true.

In step 5, we defined a `print_each_from_list` function with two definitions. The first one takes an empty list as an argument:

```
def print_each_from_list([]) do
```

The other takes a nonempty list, making the head of that list available in the h variable and the tail of that input list accessible via the t variable:

```
def print_each_from_list([h|t]) do
```

The `print_each_from_list` function is recursive. When invoked with a nonempty list as an argument, it will print the head (h) element and invoke itself again, passing the remainder of the list (t). Recursion stops when an empty list is passed and the `:ok` atom is returned. Pattern matching is used to decide which function body to execute: the first one with an empty list or the second one with a nonempty list.

Pattern matching and guard clauses in function definitions prevent us from using test cases inside functions to determine and enforce the type or the value of function arguments and acting accordingly:

```
def randomize(low, high) when low < high do
    (...)
end
```

If we omit the when low < high condition in the function definition, the function gets executed even if low is bigger than high. In this case, to ensure proper execution, we would need to compare low and high inside the function definition. Using guard clauses, we prevent the function from being executed if the defined preconditions are not met.

5
Processes and Nodes

This chapter will cover the following recipes:

- ▶ Sending messages between processes
- ▶ Making code run on all available CPUs
- ▶ Using tasks to perform multiple concurrent computations
- ▶ Creating a stateful server process (messages with counters)
- ▶ Using agents as an abstraction around states
- ▶ Using an ETS table to share the state
- ▶ Creating named nodes
- ▶ Connecting nodes
- ▶ Executing code in a different node

Introduction

In this chapter, our recipes will make use of nodes and processes. We will see how message passing takes a key role in making it possible to distribute our applications and how seamlessly we can interchange information between running processes in the same virtual machine or between processes in different virtual machines that may even be running on different physical machines. We will focus on the concepts of maintaining the state in a process or sharing it between processes with ETS tables. We will also focus on how to perform asynchronous computations using the `Tasks` module.

Sending messages between processes

In Elixir, communication between processes is performed via message passing. Each process has a mailbox where messages from the "outside" world are placed, waiting to be processed. Once that happens, if a response is required, another message will be sent, and another mailbox will get a message!

Getting ready

To get started, go to the code repository where the `messages.ex` file is located and open a new IEx terminal session. The IEx terminal session will also be an actor in this recipe! We will send messages from it to the process containing the code defined in the module.

How to do it...

Follow these steps to send messages between processes:

1. Once our session is started, load and compile the `messages.ex` module:

   ```
   iex(1)> c "messages.ex"
   [Messages]
   ```

2. Next, spawn a new process containing the code from our module:

   ```
   iex(2)> {:ok, pid} = Messages.start_link
   {:ok, #PID<0.61.0>}
   ```

3. To make things easier, we will register our newly spawned process with a name:

   ```
   iex(4)> Process.register(pid, :messages)
   true
   ```

4. Now it's time to send some messages to the process:

   ```
   iex(4)> send :messages, {"hello", self()}
   What do you mean? I'm only listening to pings and pongs!
   {"hello", #PID<0.53.0>}
   iex(5)> send :messages, {"what", self()}
   What do you mean? I'm only listening to pings and pongs!
   {"what", #PID<0.53.0>}
   iex(6)> send :messages, {"ping", self()}
   So ping to you too!
   {"ping", #PID<0.53.0>}
   iex(7)> send :messages, {"pong", self()}
   ```

```
So pong to you too!
{"pong", #PID<0.53.0>}
iex(8)> send :messages, {"pong", self()}
So pong to you too!
{"pong", #PID<0.53.0>}
iex(9)> send :messages, {"ping", self()}
So ping to you too!
{"ping", #PID<0.53.0>}
iex(10)> send :messages, {"bye", self()}
What do you mean? I'm only listening to pings and pongs!
{"bye", #PID<0.53.0>}
iex(11)> flush
"what?"
"what?"
"ping"
"pong"
"pong"
"ping"
"what?"
:ok
iex(12)>
```

5. It seems like nothing was sent back, but that's not true. On the 11th command (highlighted), we invoked `flush` to see the terminal session mailbox, and all the received messages (sent from our messenger process) are there!

> In the *Getting help and accessing documentation within IEx* recipe in *Chapter 1, Command Line*, we saw how it was possible to get access to the documentation for any module or function in the terminal. To get more information on the `flush` command, you can enter `h flush` in your IEx session.

How it works...

After compiling our module and making it available in the terminal session in step 2, we entered `{:ok, pid}` = `Messages.start_link`; this invokes the `start_link` function in the `Messages` module:

```
def start_link do
```

```
    {:ok, spawn_link(fn -> wait_for_messages() end)}
  end
```

This function returns a tuple with the `:ok` atom and the **process ID (PID)** for the spawned process; the PID is a process identifier that allows us to refer to any process. We can use the PID to send messages to that process.

In step 3, we registered the process. The PID (`#PID<0.61.0>`) was registered with the `:messages` name. This allows us to refer to the process with a registered name instead of using a PID.

In step 4, we send several messages with different contents to our messages process, calling `send :messages, {"what", self()}`. The `:messages` name is our registered reference to the spawned process and `self()` is the PID for the terminal session. The command could be generically described in the following way:

send <to_pid>, {<message>, <from_pid>}

The output we see in the console (lines 4 to 10) are not messages returned by the process, but only calls to the `IO.puts` function in order to give us some feedback on the terminal.

In step 5, when we invoke the `flush` command, we get to see the content of the terminal mailbox. Every process has its own mailbox where incoming messages are stored, and it is the place where we find all the messages our spawned process sent back as a response to the messages sent from the terminal.

There's more...

The `spawn_link` function in the `Messages` module initialization accepts a function; in this case, we defined it as `wait_for_messages`:

```
defp wait_for_messages() do
  receive do
    {"ping", caller} ->
      IO.puts "So ping to you too!"
      send caller, "ping"
      wait_for_messages()

    {"pong", caller} ->
      IO.puts "So pong to you too!"
      send caller, "pong"
      wait_for_messages()

    {_, caller} ->
      IO.puts "What do you mean? I'm only listening to pings and
pongs!"
      send caller, "what?"
```

```
        wait_for_messages()
    end
end
```

This function has a `receive` block that pattern matches the received message and then, according to the received message, prints something to the standard output, responds with a message back to the caller process, and recursively calls itself so that it can wait for the next incoming message.

Making code run on all available CPUs

You may wonder, given the name of the recipe, whether there is some special form of coding that allows Elixir to take advantage of all available processors in a machine. There isn't!

The Erlang VM, which is the VM where our Elixir programs run, takes care of it for us. It has a scheduler that is responsible for assigning computations to each of the available processors.

Getting ready

In this recipe, we will be starting the IEx session with different options regarding the scheduler, and we will run a small program that will spawn four calculations.

We will execute the program in an IEx session with the default options for the scheduler (usually one scheduler per CPU), and we will then repeat the execution in a shell started with only one enabled scheduler.

To start, we need to get into the directory where the `multiple_calculations.ex` module is located.

How to do it...

Follow these steps to see how the Erlang VM scheduler takes care of distributing computations through the available CPUs:

1. Start IEx:

   ```
   > iex

   Erlang/OTP 17 [erts-6.2] [source] [64-bit] [smp:4:4] [async-
   threads:10] [hipe] [kernel-poll:false] [dtrace]
   ```

2. Load and compile the module and execute the `start` function:

   ```
   iex(1)> c "multiple_calculations.ex"

   [MultipleCalculations]

   iex(2)> MultipleCalculations.start

   :ok
   ```

```
Sum of the squares of all odd numbers divisible by 13 between 1
and 10000000 is 12820474358991153855
```

time: 4758 ms

```
Sum of the squares of all odd numbers divisible by 13 between 1
and 20000000 is 102564194871779230759
```

time: 8286 ms

```
Sum of the squares of all odd numbers divisible by 13 between 1
and 30000000 is 346153707692261153854
```

time: 10848 ms

```
Sum of the squares of all odd numbers divisible by 13 between 1
and 40000000 is 820513558974493846150
```

time: 13347 ms

iex(3)>

3. Now, initialize another IEx session, disabling multiprocessor support:

```
> iex --erl "-smp disable"
```

```
Erlang/OTP 17 [erts-6.2] [source] [64-bit] [async-threads:10]
[hipe] [kernel-poll:false] [dtrace]
```

 The information about the shell has no reference to [smp:4:4; this means that the session has no multiprocessor support.

4. Load and compile the module and execute the start function:

```
iex(1)> c "multiple_calculations.ex"
```

[MultipleCalculations]

```
iex(2)> MultipleCalculations.start
```

:ok

```
Sum of the squares of all odd numbers divisible by 13 between 1
and 10000000 is 12820474358991153855
```

time: 8453 ms

```
Sum of the squares of all odd numbers divisible by 13 between 1
and 20000000 is 102564194871779230759
```

time: 14944 ms

```
Sum of the squares of all odd numbers divisible by 13 between 1
and 30000000 is 346153707692261153854
```

time: 19114 ms

```
Sum of the squares of all odd numbers divisible by 13 between 1
and 40000000 is 820513558974493846150

time: 21338 ms

iex(3)>
```

How it works...

The code defined inside the `multiple_calculations.ex` module spawns four processes to perform some time-consuming tasks (the description of these tasks is in the program's output).

The exact same code executed on a terminal session with the default settings for the scheduler (one per physical CPU), and in another with multiprocessing disabled, has a different performance in terms of the execution speed.

When one scheduler per CPU is enabled, the tasks are completed faster, because the VM can assign each of these tasks to all available processors. However, we do not have to worry about that in our code.

The next screenshots show you the load charts per CPU in both scenarios:

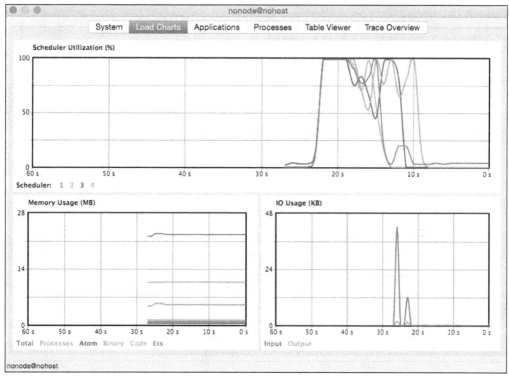

Schedulers in use

In the following screenshot, we see the SMP-disabled one scheduler in use:

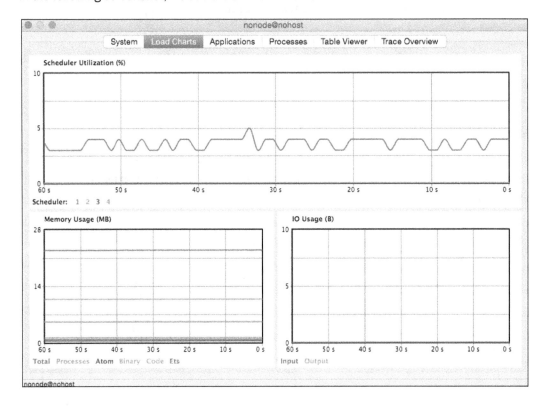

If we compare the execution times for each of the four computations, we can see how execution times increase in the shell instance that uses a single CPU core:

Computation (range)	Execution time with 4 cores	Execution time with 1 core
1..10000000	4758 ms	8453 ms
1..20000000	8286 ms	14944 ms
1..30000000	10848 ms	19114 ms
1..40000000	11347 ms	21338 ms
Total time	35239 ms	63849 ms

There's more...

The fact that the virtual machine takes care of scheduling using all the available processors doesn't mean that we shouldn't care about our code performance.

Using tasks to perform multiple concurrent computations

In this recipe, we will build a simple geolocation app that receives a list of IP addresses and outputs the country where the IP is registered. We will use Elixir's `Task` module to spawn one process per IP address in the list. The determination of the location will be performed concurrently.

The `Task` module in Elixir provides a simple abstraction for the use of processes with the purpose of performing one action during their life cycle. Normally, tasks are used when there is no need to perform communication between processes, and are a very powerful tool to help parallelize computation.

Getting ready

We will generate a Mix application, add the `geolix` application as a dependency, and also download a free IP database and configure the application to use it. We will also create two functions to geolocate the IPs: one sequential and another concurrent.

Let's get started:

1. Generate a Mix application:

```
> mix new geolocation_with_tasks --sup
* creating README.md
* creating .gitignore
* creating mix.exs
* creating config
* creating config/config.exs
* creating lib
* creating lib/geolocation_with_tasks.ex
* creating test
* creating test/test_helper.exs
* creating test/geolocation_with_tasks_test.exs

Your mix project was created successfully.
You can use mix to compile it, test it, and more:

    cd geolocation_with_tasks
    mix test

Run `mix help` for more commands.
```

2. Download the free **GeoLite2 Country** database from `http://dev.maxmind.com/` `geoip/geoip2/geolite2/`:

Dev Home   minFraud   GeoIP   Proxy Detection   FAQ   Main Site   Site Map

GeoLite2 Free Downloadable Databases

Databases

GeoLite2 databases are free IP geolocation databases comparable to, but less accurate than, MaxMind's GeoIP2 databases. GeoLite2 databases are updated on the first Tuesday of each month.

Support

MaxMind does not provide official support for the free GeoLite2 databases. If you have questions about the GeoLite2 databases or GeoIP2 APIs, please see stackoverflow's GeoIP questions and answers.

License

The GeoLite2 databases are distributed under the Creative Commons Attribution-ShareAlike 3.0 Unported License. The attribution requirement may be met by including the following in all advertising and documentation mentioning features of or use of this database:

```
This product includes GeoLite2 data created by MaxMind, available from
<a href="http://www.maxmind.com">http://www.maxmind.com</a>.
```

We also offer commercial redistribution licensing.

Downloads

Database	MaxMind DB **binary, gzipped**	CSV format, **zipped**
GeoLite2 City	Download (md5 checksum)	Download (md5 checksum)
GeoLite2 Country	Download (md5 checksum)	Download (md5 checksum)

The GeoLite2 databases may also be downloaded and updated with our GeoIP Update program.

MaxMind APIs

See GeoIP2 downloadable databases for a list of available APIs. GeoIP2 APIs may be used with GeoLite2 databases.

3. Create the `geo_db` directory inside the code directory of this chapter and unzip the file downloaded in step 2 to that location. You should have a file named `GeoLite2-Country.mmdb` inside `geolocation_with_tasks/geo_db`.

4. Add the `geolix` application as a dependency:

(File mix.exs)

```
defp deps do
  [
    { :geolix, github: "mneudert/geolix" }
  ]
end
```

5. Configure the application to start `geolix` automatically:

    (File mix.exs)

    ```
    def application do
      [applications: [:logger, :geolix],
        mod: {GeolocationWithTasks, []}]
    end
    ```

6. Get and compile the dependencies:

    ```
    > mix do deps.get, compile
    ```

7. Configure the location of the file containing the geolocation information (downloaded in step 2):

    (File config/config.exs)

    ```
    use Mix.Config

    config :geolix,
      databases: [
        { :country, "./geo_db/GeoLite2-Country.mmdb" }
      ]
    ```

How to do it...

To use the `Task` module to perform concurrent computations, follow these steps:

1. Create a file named `lib/geolocator.ex` and insert the following code:

    ```
    defmodule Geolocator do

    @ip_list [ "216.58.209.227", "199.16.156.198", "213.13.146.138",
    "114.134.80.162", "134.170.188.221", "216.58.210.3"]

      def concurrent(ip_list \\ @ip_list) when is_list ip_list do
        ip_list
        |> Enum.map(fn(ip) ->
          Task.async(fn -> ip |> locate end)
        end)
        |> Enum.map(&Task.await/1)
      end

      def sequential(ip_list \\ @ip_list) when is_list ip_list do
        Enum.map(ip_list, fn(x) -> locate(x) end)
    ```

```
        end

        def locate(ip) do
          case Geolix.lookup(ip) do
            %{country: country} ->
              location = get_in(country, [:country, :names, :en])
              IO.puts "IP: #{ip}  Country: #{location}"
            _ ->
              IO.puts "Could not determine the location of IP #{ip}"
          end
        end

    end
```

2. Start the application:

   ```
   > iex -S mix
   ```

3. Start by determining the location of each IP using the `sequential` function defined in the previous step:

   ```
   iex(1)> Geolocator.sequential
   IP: 216.58.209.227  Country: United States
   IP: 199.16.156.198  Country: United States
   IP: 213.13.146.138  Country: Portugal
   IP: 114.134.80.162  Country: Hong Kong
   IP: 134.170.188.221  Country: United States
   IP: 216.58.210.3  Country: United States
   [:ok, :ok, :ok, :ok, :ok, :ok]
   ```

4. Now, perform the same task using the function that makes use of the `Task` module:

   ```
   iex(2)> Geolocator.concurrent
   IP: 199.16.156.198  Country: United States
   IP: 216.58.209.227  Country: United States
   IP: 134.170.188.221  Country: United States
   IP: 114.134.80.162  Country: Hong Kong
   IP: 213.13.146.138  Country: Portugal
   IP: 216.58.210.3  Country: United States
   [:ok, :ok, :ok, :ok, :ok, :ok]
   ```

5. Run it once more to see the order of the results change:

```
iex(3)> Geolocator.concurrent
IP: 199.16.156.198   Country: United States
IP: 213.13.146.138   Country: Portugal
IP: 216.58.210.3   Country: United States
IP: 216.58.209.227   Country: United States
IP: 114.134.80.162   Country: Hong Kong
IP: 134.170.188.221   Country: United States
[:ok, :ok, :ok, :ok, :ok, :ok]
```

How it works...

In step 1, we create the module to perform the geolocation task.

We start by defining a list of IP addresses (@ip_list). This allows us to invoke both the concurrent and sequential functions, passing no arguments. The @ip_list is used as a default argument for both functions. In both functions, we also make use of guards (when is_list ip_list) to make sure the functions are only executed when a list is passed as an argument.

We also define two functions that behave distinctly. The sequential function will take each element of the list and sequentially invoke the locate function. No matter how many times we execute Geolocator.sequential, the output never changes.

In the concurrent function, we introduce tasks:

```
 6  def concurrent(ip_list \\ @ip_list) when is_list ip_list do
 7    ip_list
 8    |> Enum.map(fn(ip)->
 9        Task.async(fn -> ip |> locate end)
10      end)
11    |> Enum.map(&Task.await/1)
12  end
```

The code flow is this: we pass ip_list as a collection to the Enum.map function in line 8. The anonymous function we use to map the collection is Task.async(fn -> ip |> locate end). This function is the one that performs the call to the locate/1 function. We then map the resulting collection again with the &Task.await/1 anonymous function (line 11). This is in order to actually wait for the results from the computations performed by each task. Doing this allows us to get the status of the computation. Both in steps 4 and 5, the last line is the following:

[:ok, :ok, :ok, :ok, :ok, :ok]

The `Task.await` function allows us to view the return value, informing us of the success of each operation. If we commented out line 11, our output would be something like this:

```
[%Task{pid: #PID<0.212.0>, ref: #Reference<0.0.0.1356>},
 %Task{pid: #PID<0.213.0>, ref: #Reference<0.0.0.1357>},
 %Task{pid: #PID<0.214.0>, ref: #Reference<0.0.0.1358>},
 %Task{pid: #PID<0.215.0>, ref: #Reference<0.0.0.1359>},
 %Task{pid: #PID<0.216.0>, ref: #Reference<0.0.0.1360>},
 %Task{pid: #PID<0.217.0>, ref: #Reference<0.0.0.1361>}]
```

This means that although each task is executed, the process that spawned them has no way to access the status of each task.

In step 3, we execute the `sequential` function that processes each entry in the list in an order. It takes each element, performs the computation, and returns the result. As long as the list doesn't change, the order of the processing will be the same.

As we can see in steps 4 and 5, when using the `concurrent` function, the output changes. Each element of the list gets assigned to a process (task), and the execution occurs in parallel. This is the reason we cannot determine the order of the results and they actually change every time the function is executed.

There's more...

Elixir tasks can also be spawned inside a supervision tree using the `start_link/1` and `start_link/3` functions. However, remember that once supervised, tasks cannot be waited on. If they are placed in a supervision tree, they will not be linked directly to the caller, and that link is what allows a task to be waited on.

Elixir also provides the `Task.Supervisor` module to allow starting supervisors that dynamically supervise tasks.

We will be looking into supervisors in the *Creating a supervisor* recipe in *Chapter 6, OTP – Open Telecom Platform*, but you can find more information on the `Task` and `Task.Supervisor` modules in the Elixir documentation at `http://elixir-lang.org/docs/stable/elixir/Task.html` and `http://elixir-lang.org/docs/stable/elixir/Task.Supervisor.html`.

Creating a stateful server process (messages with counters)

In this recipe, we will use the same concept used in the first recipe, but we will add a counter for each type of received message. We will introduce states!

Getting ready

To get started, let's create a module named `messages_with_state.ex` with the following code:

```elixir
defmodule MessagesWithState do

  def start_link do
    {:ok, spawn_link(fn -> wait_for_messages(0,0,0) end)}
  end

  defp wait_for_messages(pings, pongs, unknown) do
    receive do
      {"ping", caller} ->
        send caller, "pong"
        IO.puts "Received #{pings + 1} ping messages!"
        wait_for_messages(pings + 1, pongs, unknown)

      {"pong", caller} ->
        send caller, "pong"
        IO.puts "Received #{pongs + 1} pong messages!"
        wait_for_messages(pings, pongs + 1, unknown)

      {:status, _caller} ->
        IO.puts "Current status: #{pings} pings, #{pongs} pongs
          and #{unknown} unknown messages."

      {_, caller} ->
        IO.puts "What do you mean? I have received #{unknown + 1}
          unknown messages!"
        send caller, "unknown"
        wait_for_messages(pings, pongs, unknown + 1)
    end
  end
end
```

This code is very similar to the one we used in the `messages.ex` module in the first recipe of this chapter, which is the *Sending messages between processes* recipe. We are just enhancing it with the ability to hold states! We will keep a counter that will increase by one when a new message is received.

How to do it...

Follow these steps to see our process maintain a counter of the received messages:

1. We will start by loading the module and registering the process with a name, in this case, `:message_server`:

   ```
   iex(1)> c "messages_with_state.ex"
   [MessagesWithState]
   iex(2)> {:ok, pid} = MessagesWithState.start_link
   {:ok, #PID<0.61.0>}
   iex(3)> Process.register(pid, :message_server)
   true
   ```

2. We will now send some messages to our server:

   ```
   iex(4)> send :message_server, {"ping", self()}
   Received 1 ping messages!
   iex(5)> send :message_server, {"ping", self()}
   Received 2 ping messages!
   iex(6)> send :message_server, {"pong", self()}
   Received 1 pong messages!
   iex(7)> send :message_server, {"what", self()}
   What do you mean? I have received 1 unknown messages!
   iex(8)> send :message_server, {"what", self()}
   What do you mean? I have received 2 unknown messages!
   iex(9)> send :message_server, {"ping", self()}
   Received 3 ping messages!
   iex(10)> send :message_server, {:status, self()}
   Current status: 3 pings, 1 pongs and 2 unknown messages.
   ```

How it works...

When we modified our `messages` module, we added three arguments to the `wait_for_messages` function:

```
defp wait_for_messages(pings, pongs, unknown) do (...)
```

These arguments are initialized with the 0 value when the server is spawned:

```
def start_link do
  {:ok, spawn_link(fn -> wait_for_messages(0,0,0) end)}
end
```

Then, in each recursive call after receiving a message (lines 11, 16, and 24), we need to pass the current state in the form of these three arguments:

```
wait_for_messages(pings, pongs + 1, unknown)
wait_for_messages(pings + 1, pongs, unknown)
wait_for_messages(pings, pongs, unknown + 1)
```

In the previous lines, depending on the type of message received, we update the counter for that type of message and call the same function recursively, feeding the updated values for the message counters.

There is no global state and each spawned process has its own state that has to be passed between function calls in order to be updated or maintained.

For those more used to object-oriented languages, this option may seem odd, but remember that it is this insulation of states between processes that allows a simpler and effective concurrency model.

See also

▶ In the *Using agents as an abstraction around states* and *Using an ETS table to share states* recipes, we will discuss the use of a placeholder for the state that needs to be shared between processes

Using agents as an abstraction around states

The `Agent` module provides a basic server implementation and is a convenient way to spawn a process that needs to maintain a state. Agents in Elixir provide an intuitive API to update and retrieve the state.

In this recipe, we will create a module, `phone_book.ex`, where we will be able to store and retrieve data.

How to do it...

To create our phone book using an agent to maintain states, follow these steps:

1. Open your code editor and create a file named `phone_book.ex`.

2. Add the following code to the file you created:

```
defmodule PhoneBook do

    @name __MODULE__

    def start_link do
```

```
        Agent.start_link(fn -> %{} end, name: @name)
      end

      def insert(user, number) do
        Agent.update(@name, &Map.put(&1, user, number))
      end

      def get(user) do
        Agent.get(@name, &Map.get(&1, user))
      end

    end
```

3. Start IEx and load the module:

   > **iex phone_book.ex**

4. Start the process that will hold our phone book data:

   iex(1)> PhoneBook.start_link

   {:ok, #PID<0.59.0>}

5. Insert some numbers into the phone book:

   iex(2)> PhoneBook.insert(:bob, "111-22-333-444")

   :ok

   iex(3)> PhoneBook.insert(:joe, "111-99-999-999")

   :ok

6. Retrieve data from the phone book:

   iex(4)> PhoneBook.get(:joe)

   "111-99-999-999"

7. Update the value retrieved in the previous step:

   iex(5)> PhoneBook.insert(:joe, "111-88-333-888")

   :ok

8. Get the value once more to verify that the changes persisted:

   iex(6)> PhoneBook.get(:joe)

   "111-88-333-888"

How it works...

With 12 lines of code, we were able to define a module that allows the insertion and retrieval of data, thus maintaining the state. For this purpose, we used Elixir's `Agent` module.

We start the agent in step 4 by passing an anonymous function that initializes an empty map (`%{}`) and registers the agent with a name; in this case, the name is defined using `@name` and by assigning it `__MODULE__`:

```
Agent.start_link(fn -> %{} end, name: @name)
```

This means that the agent will be registered with the name of the module (`PhoneBook`) and will be accessible by name without the need to use the PID. The empty map is the initial state of the process.

> The return value is `{:ok, #PID<0.59.0>}`. Even though we registered the process with a name, we can access it using this PID.

In steps 5 and 7, we use the `insert` function to update the phone book (and the state of the process). This is achieved using the `Agent.update` function:

```
Agent.update(@name, &Map.put(&1, user, number))
```

We pass the name under which the process is registered as the first argument, and the second argument is the function to update the state. Here, we get the map that holds the state of the agent and insert (put) the user and number.

> Take a look at the following code:
> ```
> &Map.put(&1, user, number)
> ```
> It is equivalent to the following:
> ```
> fn(map) -> Map.put(map, user, number) end
> ```

In steps 6 and 8, we use the `Agent.get` function to get the current values stored in the process. This function is very similar to the `update` function, but it only takes two arguments: the map representing the state of the process and the key we wish to retrieve from that map:

```
Agent.get(@name, &Map.get(&1, user))
```

There's more...

Although limited in comparison to a full-blown GenServer, agents are simple to use and allow us to quickly spawn a process in order to maintain states. In the next chapter, we will focus on OTP, and we will use the GenServer behavior that serves as the foundation of the agent implementation.

Using an ETS table to share the state

In the *Creating a stateful server process (messages with counters)* and *Using agents as an abstraction around states* recipes, we saw that in order to maintain the state in our processes, we had to be passing the function calls to the state.

This solves the problem when a process needs to maintain states, but what if we need to share some data between multiple processes?

One of the solutions is the use of a structure that allows concurrent access and is really effective in the retrieval of data. This structure is called ETS.

 ETS means **Erlang Term Storage**, and it is an in-memory store.

In this recipe, we will create a small wrapper around an ETS table that can be used as a **key/value** store.

Getting ready

To create our key/value store, let's create new module `ets_store.ex` and add the following code:

```
defmodule EtsStore do
  @table_id __MODULE__

  def init do
    :ets.new(@table_id, [:public, :named_table])
  end

  def insert(key, value) do
    :ets.insert(@table_id, {key, value})
  end

  def get(key) do
    case :ets.lookup(@table_id, key) do
      [{_key, value}]  -> {:ok, value}
      []               -> {:error, :not_found}
    end
  end

  def delete(key) do
```

```
        :ets.match_delete(@table_id, {key, :_})
    end

end
```

How to do it...

We will use our newly defined module to store values that are accessible by any process. The steps are as follows:

1. Open a new IEx session and load the `ets_store` module:

    iex(1)> c "ets_store.ex"

    [EtsStore]

2. Initialize the `EtsStore` module:

    iex(2)> EtsStore.init

    EtsStore

3. Now we can use it to store some values:

    iex(3)> EtsStore.insert(:one, 1)

    iex(4)> EtsStore.insert("two", 2)

    iex(5)> EtsStore.insert(:two, 2)

    iex(6)> EtsStore.insert(:three, "three")

4. We can also use it to retrieve values:

    iex(7)> EtsStore.get("two")

    {:ok, 2}

    iex(8)> EtsStore.get(:two)

    {:ok, 2}

5. We can also delete entries from it:

    iex(9)> EtsStore.delete("two")

    true

6. The Observer tool is really helpful in order to visualize the state of any ETS table; let's start it to check our store:

    iex(10)> :observer.start

    :ok

7. Select the **Table Viewer** tab and double-click on **Elixir.EtsStore** to see the keys and values it currently stores:

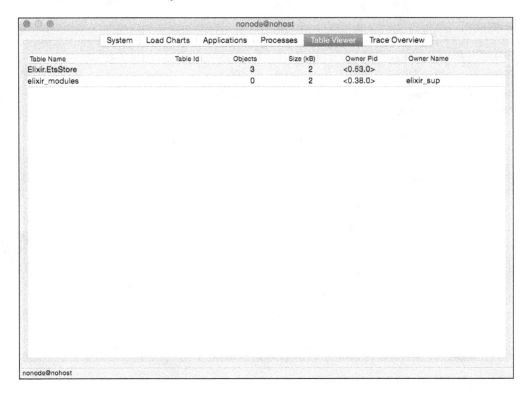

This is what the table looks like:

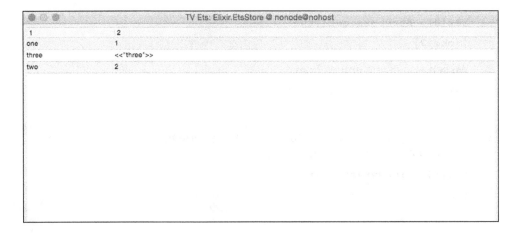

How it works...

In the `init` function for our `EtsStore` module, we call the `ets` Erlang module and pass it the name of the table and a list of options. In this case, we chose to create a public table, which means other processes may read and write to it. We also chose the option of `named_table` to allow all to refer to it by its name instead of having to use its PID reference:

```
def init do
  :ets.new(@table_id, [:public, :named_table])
end
```

 There are several other options; we can choose how the table should behave, such as `set`, `ordered_set`, `bag`, or `ordered_bag` and between different permission levels: public, protected, and private.

The other functions in our module are wrappers around the `ets` Erlang module to provide us with a more idiomatic way of interaction.

There's more...

The owning process of this ETS table is the terminal where we initialized it. If we close the terminal window, the table will be destroyed.

In some cases, this behavior makes sense, but if desired, an ETS may even be part of a supervision tree and its ownership may be passed between processes.

Creating named nodes

Until now, we have been using our IEx sessions without naming them. You may notice this because the prompt for the IEx terminal session only has this indication: `iex(1)>`. The IEx session is a node, and if we run two or more different nodes, even on the same machine, we are running multiple instances of the Erlang virtual machine.

Using two nodes on the same machine or two nodes on different machines is exactly the same thing, apart from connection latency, and that is why there is a need to connect them securely.

By executing several nodes, we are paving the way for distribution and fault tolerance. At this point, we will be focusing on the task of naming our nodes to make them easier to access.

Getting ready

In this recipe, we will be creating nodes with a short name and with a full name as well. Usually, short names are the option when the nodes are in the same network, and long names are the option when we need to create nodes that will interconnect within different networks.

We will start by opening a terminal window in order to create our named nodes.

How to do it...

To create named nodes, follow these steps:

1. Let's first check what is happening when no name is specified for a node when we start an IEx session:

   ```
   > iex

   Interactive Elixir (1.0.2) - press Ctrl+C to exit (type h() ENTER
   for help)

   iex(1)>
   ```

2. No information about the node is displayed in the IEx prompt. Let's try to figure out what the current node name is:

   ```
   iex(1)> Node.self

   :nonode@nohost
   ```

3. Now, let's exit the session by pressing *Ctrl + C* twice and start a new session, naming our node. We will use the short name option:

   ```
   > iex --sname "cookbook"

   Interactive Elixir (1.0.2) - press Ctrl+C to exit (type h() ENTER
   for help)

   iex(cookbook@pap-macbook)1>
   ```

4. Let's exit once more and this time, start the node with a fully qualified name:

   ```
   > iex --name "cookbook@127.0.0.1"

   Interactive Elixir (1.0.2) - press Ctrl+C to exit (type h() ENTER
   for help)

   iex(cookbook@127.0.0.1)1>
   ```

How it works...

When we start our nodes (IEx sessions are nodes) without specifying a name, our node is already named. The default name is :nonode@nohost.

To be able to connect nodes in the same machine, we don't need the IP address (or the hostname), so we usually go for the `sname` option. The short name allows us to indicate the name of the node, and then the machine name will be appended, as we observed in step 3.

When we need to connect nodes in different machines, we have to indicate the IP or hostname. In step 4, we use the `name` option. This allows us to assign a fully qualified name to our node. This way, it's possible to identify it and connect to it from another machine.

See also

▸   In the *Connecting nodes* and *Executing code in another node* recipes of this chapter, we will be using the options that are presented.

Connecting nodes

In this recipe, we will start two different terminal sessions that will be our nodes, and we will connect them.

Getting ready

We will need two terminal windows opened and in each of them, we will create a node.

How to do it...

1. Start a named node in terminal window one:

   ```
   > iex --name one@127.0.0.1
   Interactive Elixir (1.0.2) - press Ctrl+C to exit (type h() ENTER
   for help)
   iex(one@127.0.0.1)1>
   ```

2. Start another named node in terminal window two:

   ```
   > iex --name two@127.0.0.1
   Interactive Elixir (1.0.2) - press Ctrl+C to exit (type h() ENTER
   for help)
   iex(two@127.0.0.1)1>
   ```

3. Verify the list of nodes that each of our newly created nodes is aware of:

   ```
   iex(one@127.0.0.1)1> Node.list
   []
   iex(two@127.0.0.1)1> Node.list
   []
   ```

4. To connect the two nodes, we will just need to instruct one of them to perform the connection:

```
iex(one@127.0.0.1)2> Node.connect :"two@127.0.0.1"
true
```

5. Now, confirm that both nodes are connected and aware of each other:

```
iex(one@127.0.0.1)3> Node.list
[:"two@127.0.0.1"]
iex(two@127.0.0.1)2> Node.list
[:"one@127.0.0.1"]
```

How it works...

In steps 1 and 2, we created nodes using the `--name` option (a fully qualified name), passing the name of the node and the IP of the machine.

In step 3, we confirmed that although running in the same machine, nodes are not automatically aware of the presence of other nodes.

To connect both nodes, in step 4, we only needed to instruct one of them to connect to the other, and they became aware of one another. We confirmed this in step 5 when we issued the `Node.list` command.

There's more...

When connecting nodes in the same machine, a cookie file (such as `.erlang.cookie`) is usually created and placed in the user root path. Both nodes may read from that file and use the value defined there.

To connect nodes in different machines, it is necessary to specify the value for `--cookie` when the named node is started. As an example, consider the following:

```
> iex --name mynode@my-ip-address --cookie mycookietext
```

All nodes we wish to connect must provide the same value for the cookie.

 Be aware that when you are setting the cookie to connect nodes in two different machines, it will be transmitted in plain text.

▸ In the *Executing code in a different node* recipe, we will connect two nodes and perform the execution of a function defined in node one in node two

Executing code in a different node

It is possible to define a function in a node and execute it in another one.

In this recipe, we will be connecting two nodes and will define a function to print a greeting message with the greeter name (in this case, the node's full name). Afterwards, we will execute the function in both nodes!

Getting ready

To be able to execute a function in another node, we will start by following the steps from the previous recipe. We will create two nodes and connect them together. Repeat the steps from the previous recipe to get started.

How to do it...

With both nodes up and running and connected, we are ready to start:

1. Define a function in node one:

```
iex(one@127.0.0.1)4> greeting_node = fn() -> IO.puts("Hello from
#{inspect(Node.self)}") end
#Function<20.90072148/0 in :erl_eval.expr/5>
```

2. It's time to instruct the second node to run the function we defined in node one:

```
iex(one@127.0.0.1)21> Node.spawn(:"two@127.0.0.1", greeting_node)
#PID<9007.76.0>
Hello from :"two@127.0.0.1"
ok
```

3. To make sure node two is not aware of the function, we will try to execute it there as well:

```
iex(two@127.0.0.1)5> Node.spawn(:"two@127.0.0.1", greeting_node)
** (RuntimeError) undefined function: greeting_node/0
```

How it works...

The function we defined in step 1 prints the result of the `inspect` function applied in a node (`Node.self`).

In step 2, we use the `Node.spawn` function that accepts a node and a function as arguments. A new process responsible for running the function will be spawned in the given node.

As a result, we get a PID as the output, and then the message is printed on the caller node with the greeting message from the node that actually executed the code (`two@127.0.0.1`).

In step 3, we made sure that node two doesn't have the `greeting_function` function defined.

There's more...

This simple example highlights one of the strengths of Elixir and the underlying Erlang platform: code may be executed in any node as if it were local. We already saw in the *Making code run on all available CPUs* recipe that a code with no changes was run either by one or multiple processors, and now we got to see that even a different node, in the same machine or in another one, can execute code that's defined elsewhere.

6
OTP – Open Telecom Platform

This chapter will cover the following recipes:

- ▶ Implementing a GenServer
- ▶ Expanding our server
- ▶ Creating a supervisor
- ▶ Using Observer to inspect supervisors and processes
- ▶ Handling errors and managing exceptions
- ▶ Packaging and releasing an OTP application
- ▶ Deploying applications and updating a running system

Introduction

Open Telecom Platform (**OTP**) is a set of libraries created by Ericsson as a systematization of common Erlang programming concepts.

The process-oriented nature of Erlang (and Elixir by extension) provides an immense power that may sometimes lead to strange problems. Given the concurrent nature of the languages, sometimes these problems may be really difficult to understand.

OTP was created around the concept of **behaviors**. A server will generally have the same structure. A finite state machine also has a known implementation pattern. The idea was to create a structure for each of the OTP-defined components that would allow the use of a well-defined and tested structure.

Implementing large-scale systems with a distributed and concurrent nature is much easier given the existence of OTP, which provides a good foundation for these systems.

In this chapter, we will be looking into some of the behaviors available in Elixir (**Application**, **GenServer**, and **Supervisor**).

In the previous chapter, we used tasks and agents, These are two abstractions provided on top of OTP.

Implementing a GenServer

In this recipe, we will implement a simple server that will store pairs of values (IP and UUID). This might be used, for instance, to store users of a system who are currently connected.

In this recipe, we will only store the provided information and respond to requests on whether a user with a given IP is connected or not.

Getting ready

We will implement a server using the OTP-defined GenServer behavior. We will need to implement the `start_link` and `init` functions and some callbacks to handle the messages our server receives (`handle_call` or `handle_cast`). To make the interaction with the server more pleasant, we will create some wrappers around the callbacks creating a client API.

>
> The GenServer-defined behavior enforces the separation between client and server. An example of it is the fact that `start_link/3` happens in the client, while `init/1` is its counterpart callback that runs on the server.
>
> The `handle_call` callback is a handler for synchronous calls while `handle_cast` is a handler for asynchronous calls. As a rule of thumb, `handle_call` is used when a response from the server is expected whereas `handle_cast` is used when no response is expected or we don't want to block while waiting for a response.

Our server will be defined in the `connection_tracker.ex` file with the following code:

```
defmodule ConnectionTracker do
  use GenServer

  ## Client API
  def start_link(opts \\ []) do
    GenServer.start_link(__MODULE__, :ok, opts)
```

```
  end

  def add_user(server, message) do
    GenServer.cast(server, {:add, message})
  end

  def search_user(server, ip) do
    GenServer.call(server, {:search, ip})
  end

  ## Callbacks (Server API)
  def init(:ok) do
    {:ok, HashDict.new}
  end

  def handle_cast({:add, message}, connection_dict) do
    {ip, uuid} = message
    if HashDict.get(connection_dict, message) do
      {:noreply, connection_dict}
    else
      {:noreply, HashDict.put(connection_dict, ip, uuid)}
    end
  end

  def handle_call({:search, ip}, _from, connection_dict) do
    {:reply, HashDict.fetch(connection_dict, ip), connection_dict}
  end

end
```

How to do it...

To load our server and perform some requests, we will follow these steps:

1. Start a new IEx session and compile the module:

   ```
   > iex
   iex(1)> c "connection_tracker.ex"
   [ConnectionTracker]
   ```

2. Initialize the server:

   ```
   iex(2)> {:ok, ct} = ConnectionTracker.start_link
   {:ok, #PID<0.179.0>}
   ```

3. Store some users:

```
iex(3)> ConnectionTracker.add_user(ct, {"127.0.0.1","uuid1"})
:ok
iex(4)> ConnectionTracker.add_user(ct, {"127.0.0.2","uuid2"})
:ok
```

4. Ask the server whether a given user is registered or not:

```
iex(5)> ConnectionTracker.search_user(ct, "127.0.0.1")
{:ok, "uuid1"}
iex(6)> ConnectionTracker.search_user(ct, "0.0.0.0")
:error
iex(7)> ConnectionTracker.search_user(ct, "127.0.0.2")
{:ok, "uuid2"}
```

How it works...

After we compiled our server in step 2, we started it and, via pattern matching, we assigned its PID to the `ct` variable. This variable will be used in the calls to our server as a placeholder for the PID of the server process.

In step 3, we add users to the connection tracker server using the `add_user` function defined in the server client API section. This way, we don't need to call the server callbacks directly. Let's take a closer look at the `add_user` function:

```
def add_user(server, message) do
  GenServer.cast(server, {:add, message})
end
```

We use the `handle_cast` callback because we don't need to wait for the result of the user insertion. We pass the server PID (`server`) and a tuple (to be pattern matched in the `handle_cast` function) containing an atom that defines the type of action and a message as arguments of our `add_user` function.

The `handle_cast` implementation starts by decomposing the passed message into an IP and UUID and verifies whether the IP already exists in the dictionary (**HashDict**) containing the entries for connected users. If the entry exists, nothing is done; if not, the IP/UUID key/value pair gets inserted into the dictionary.

In step 4, we use the `search_user` function that is no more than a wrapper around `GenServer.call`. This time, we need to wait for a response so we have to go for the synchronous call!

The structure of the function and the callback is quite similar to the one explained previously. Briefly, the `search_user` function invokes `GenServer.call`. The `GenServer.call` callback then sends a message to the server process, and this message is then processed by the `handle_call` callback. The response is the result of the HashDict search for the given key.

 On both `handle_call` and `handle_cast`, the state is passed around; in this case, it is the HashDict containing the entries of the connected users. We also use the `:reply` and `:no_reply` atoms to indicate whether the server returns a message or not.

There's more...

All the OTP behaviors defined in Erlang are directly usable in Elixir. Some of these behaviors are **GenEvent**, **Supervisor**, and **Application**.

Expanding our server

Our server implementation lacks a few things. How to stop it gracefully and how to upgrade its code?

Our current implementation (right below the `## Callbacks (Server API)` comment) has three of the six callbacks that form the GenServer base skeleton. The ones missing are `handle_info/2`, `terminate/2`, and `code_change/3`.

We will be implementing all of these functions in this recipe.

 The GenServer provides default implementations for all `:gen_server` callbacks. This is the reason we can get away without having to define all of them explicitly, like we did in Erlang.

Getting ready

To start, we need to load the `connection_tracker.ex` module in a code editor.

How to do it...

We will follow these steps to implement the functions and make our server a full-blown **GenServer**:

1. Implement the `handle_info/2` function:

```
def handle_info(info, state) do
  IO.puts("Received info message #{inspect(info)}")
  {:noreply, state}
end
```

2. Implement the `terminate/2` function:

```
def terminate(reason, state) do
  IO.puts("Terminating... reason: #{inspect(reason)}")
  {:ok, state}
end
```

3. Implement the `code_change/3` function:

```
def code_change(_oldVsn, state, _extra) do
  # perform the actions to upgrade/downgrade/update code
  {:ok, state}
end
```

How it works...

We already saw the purpose of `init/1`, `handle_call/3`, and `handle_cast/2` in the previous recipe. The functions that are now implemented have their own purpose as well.

In step 1, we implemented the `init` function. This function handles messages regarding timeouts or messages not made via a synchronous or asynchronous request (call or cast). If the message was due to a timeout, the information will be the `:timeout` atom; if not, it will be the message itself. In our example, we are only printing the info message to the standard output, but we might even ignore the info message.

Step 2 consists of the `terminate` function. This function is supposed to be the counterpart of `init`. It is called when the GenServer is about to terminate and, in the same way, when we set up our state when the server was initiated and if there's any cleanup to take place, it should happen here. We could, for instance, transfer the state to another process.

The last step implements the `code_change` function. This is the function that gets called when the GenServer needs to update its internal state, be it on an upgrade or downgrade of the code. Yes, it's not a typo! You can actually update the code on a running system!

See also

- The Erlang documentation for the `gen_server` module is very detailed, and if you want to go a little deeper you can access it at `http://www.erlang.org/doc/man/gen_server.html`

- The Elixir GenServer documentation is accessible at `http://elixir-lang.org/docs/stable/elixir/GenServer.html`

Creating a supervisor

One of the main advantages of Elixir is fault tolerance, and one of the underlying philosophies is the famous *let it crash* philosophy. This means that by principle, no defensive programming is performed. You write the code that expresses your intent and handles the case you are expecting, and then if something goes wrong, you just let the process crash.

There are mechanisms in Elixir that allow the monitoring of processes and even give you the ability to relaunch a process (or a group of processes) if something goes wrong.

Probably in case of programming errors, this doesn't make sense, but what if the error was due to something that's external to your program? What if the program is logically sound, and everything is working as it's supposed to but, say, a resource, such as a network, fails? Your processes might crash because of that. What if there was a mechanism that would allow you to try again? Fortunately, there is: **supervisors**!

This is another OTP-defined behavior. A process supervises another one or more processes. The supervised processes may be supervisors or workers. The module we implemented in the last two recipes is an example of a worker module that may benefit from being supervised.

Getting ready

We will introduce a client function (`crash_the_server`) and its `handle_call` callback that will perform the division of an integer by 0:

```
# Client API
def crash_the_server(server, number) when is_integer number do
  GenServer.call(server,{:crash_me, number})
end

# Callbacks (Server API)
def handle_call({:crash_me, number}, _from, connection_dict) do
  {:reply, div(number,0), connection_dict}
end
```

This way, we may make the server crash. To see it, open an IEx session:

```
> iex
```

Load and compile the module:

```
iex(1)> c "connection_tracker.ex"
[ConnectionTracker]
```

Now, let's start the server and feed and invoke the `crash_the_server` function:

```
iex(2)> {:ok, server} = ConnectionTracker.start_link
{:ok, #PID<0.61.0>}
iex(3)> ConnectionTracker.crash_the_server(server, 9)
```

As expected, the result was not good. Our server crashed and if we enter `server` in the terminal, it no longer shows us the PID. The `server` process died!

```
                         1. iex (beam.smp)
→  supervisor git:(develop) x iex
Erlang/OTP 17 [erts-6.2] [source] [64-bit] [smp:4:4] [async-threads:10] [hipe] [kernel-p
oll:false] [dtrace]

Interactive Elixir (1.0.2) – press Ctrl+C to exit (type h() ENTER for help)
iex(1)> c "connection_tracker.ex"
[ConnectionTracker]
iex(2)> {:ok, server} = ConnectionTracker.
add_user/2            crash_the_server/2      search_user/2
start_link/1
iex(2)> {:ok, server} = ConnectionTracker.start_link
{:ok, #PID<0.61.0>}
iex(3)> ConnectionTracker.crash_the_server(server,9)
Terminating... reason: {:badarith, [{ConnectionTracker, :handle_call, 3, [file: 'connect
ion_tracker.ex', line: 37]}, {:gen_server, :handle_msg, 5, [file: 'gen_server.erl', line
: 580]}, {:proc_lib, :init_p_do_apply, 3, [file: 'proc_lib.erl', line: 237]}]}
** (EXIT from #PID<0.53.0>) an exception was raised:
    ** (ArithmeticError) bad argument in arithmetic expression
        connection_tracker.ex:37: ConnectionTracker.handle_call/3
        (stdlib) gen_server.erl:580: :gen_server.handle_msg/5
        (stdlib) proc_lib.erl:237: :proc_lib.init_p_do_apply/3

Interactive Elixir (1.0.2) – press Ctrl+C to exit (type h() ENTER for help)

23:59:47.527 [error] GenServer #PID<0.61.0> terminating
Last message: {:crash_me, 9}
State: #HashDict<[]>
** (exit) an exception was raised:
    ** (ArithmeticError) bad argument in arithmetic expression
        connection_tracker.ex:37: ConnectionTracker.handle_call/3
        (stdlib) gen_server.erl:580: :gen_server.handle_msg/5
        (stdlib) proc_lib.erl:237: :proc_lib.init_p_do_apply/3
iex(1)> server
** (RuntimeError) undefined function: server/0

iex(1)> █
```

How to do it...

To implement a supervisor that allows our server to survive calls to this wrongly implemented function, we will follow these steps:

1. Create a `connection_tracker_sup.ex` file in the same directory as the `connection_tracker` module with the "bad" function.

2. Insert this code into the file:

```
defmodule ConnectionTrackerSup do
  use Supervisor

  def start_link do
    Supervisor.start_link(__MODULE__, [], [{:name, __MODULE__}])
  end

  # supervisor callback
  def init([]) do
    child = [worker(ConnectionTracker, [], [])]
    supervise(child, [{:strategy, :one_for_one},
      {:max_restarts, 1}, {:max_seconds, 5}])
  end
end
```

How it works...

To create a supervisor, we need to add only one function: `init`.

The `start_link` function is a convenience function and not a mandatory one. However, it makes our interaction more consistent with the way the GenServer works.

The `init` function returns the child processes managed by the supervisor and the configuration for the supervision. In this case, the options are `:strategy`, `:max_restarts`, and `:max_seconds`. There are multiple possibilities for these settings. With the current code, we will respawn a process for each that crashes but we will only do it once! The last option means that the processes can crash once every five seconds without taking down the supervisor.

See also

▸   For more information on the restarting strategies and other configuration options of the `Supervisor` module, check the documentation at `http://elixir-lang.org/docs/stable/elixir/Supervisor.html`

Using Observer to inspect supervisors and processes

The Observer tool we already used in a couple of recipes throughout the book allows us to have a better insight on supervision trees and to have information on the processes. It also allows us to "kill" a process and watch it be replaced by another one!

How to do it...

To start inspecting our supervisors and processes, we will follow these steps:

1. Open a new IEx session:

    ```
    > iex
    ```

2. Start the Observer tool:

    ```
    iex(1)> :observer.start
    ```

3. Select the **Applications** tab in the graphical interface.

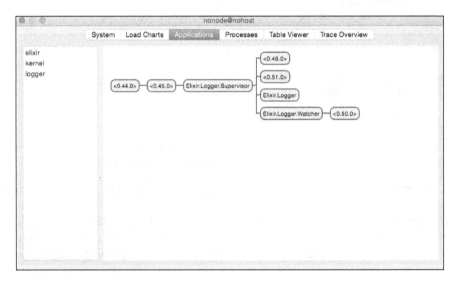

4. In the **logger** application info, right-click on **Elixir.Logger.Watcher** and select the **Kill process** option, and then confirm the option in the popup.

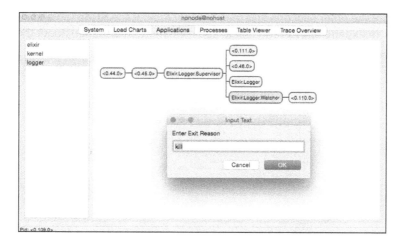

5. Take a look at the PIDs for some processes. They have changed! This means that `Elixir.Logger.Supervisor` restarted some processes when one of its supervised processes terminated.

 We are the culprits for the failure but it serves the purpose of illustrating the power of a supervision tree and how it makes the task of writing resilient systems simple!

6. Double-click on **Elixir.Logger.Supervisor** to see its properties.

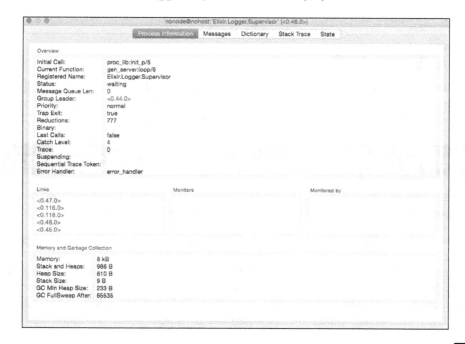

7. Explore the other sections and take a closer look at the **State** tab and click on the **Click to expand above term** link to see even more information about the supervisor.

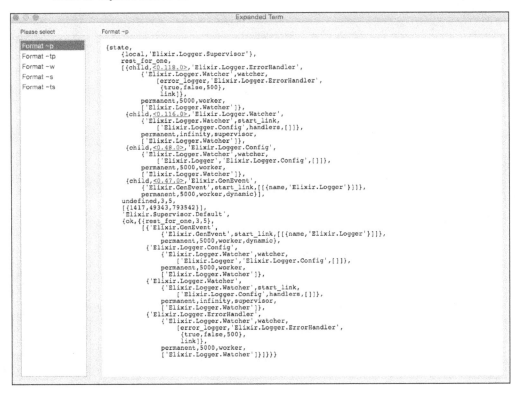

How it works...

The Observer tool allows you to access information about several aspects of a running virtual machine and not just the memory or CPU usage count. The Observer tool is a great help with inspecting individual processes and their received messages, stack contents, and so on.

Handling errors and managing exceptions

We already approached the *let it crash* mantra. We saw in the previous two recipes how an Elixir system is able to deal with failures in processes and keep running.

Defensive programming is not encouraged at all by the principles that guide languages such as Elixir or Erlang. Even if we aren't writing defensively, it is still a good idea to control what happens when errors occur. Supervisors allow us to write code that keeps breaking and crashing and yet recovers from the crash. We will mainly find two categories of errors after compiling our code (compilation errors are outside this equation): runtime errors and logic errors. The former are easier to deal with, while the latter may become more difficult to reason and track.

In distributed systems, a whole set of problems may rise due to race conditions, timing issues, network unreliability, and so on.

To track and solve this category of errors, we benefit from the ability to debug live systems via the console and actually change the running code. That's one of the reasons GenServer implements the `code_change/3` function (refer to the *Expanding our server* recipe of this chapter).

To deal with runtime errors or the more simple logical ones, Elixir offers us some possibilities: errors, throws, and exits.

In this recipe, we will be looking at each one of these possibilities.

Getting ready

Create a new file named `error_handling.ex` and add the following code:

```elixir
defmodule ErrorHandling do

  def safe_division(a, b) do
    try do
      div(a,b)
    rescue
      _error -> _error
    end
  end

  def throw_on_zero(list) do
    try do
      Enum.each list, fn(_number)-> if _number == 0, do: throw(_
number) end
      "Good! No zeros on the list!"
    catch
      _number -> "Oops! There was a #{_number} on the list!"
    end
  end

  def shortest_living_process do
    IO.puts "Spawning process..."
    spawn_link fn ->
              IO.puts "Process started!"
              exit(1)
            end
  end

end
```

Open a new IEx session and load the `error_handling.ex` module:

```
> iex
Interactive Elixir (1.0.2) - press Ctrl+C to exit (type h() ENTER for
help)
iex(1)> c "error_handling.ex"
[ErrorHandling]
iex(2)>
```

How to do it...

To see how to handle errors, we will follow these steps:

1. Call the `safe_division` function from the loaded module with a valid input and an invalid one:

   ```
   iex(3)> ErrorHandling.safe_division(2,2)

   1

   iex(3)> ErrorHandling.safe_division(2,0)

   %ArithmeticError{}
   ```

2. Call the `throw_on_zero` function, passing it a list not containing a zero, and invoke it again with a list containing a zero:

   ```
   iex(6)> ErrorHandling.throw_on_zero([1,2,3,4,5])

   "Good! No zeros on the list!"

   iex(7)> ErrorHandling.throw_on_zero([1,2,3,4,5,0])

   "Oops! There was a zero on the list!"
   ```

3. To see the exit in action invoke the `shortest_living_process` function:

   ```
   iex(9)> ErrorHandling.shortest_living_process

   Spawning process...

   Process started!

   ** (EXIT from #PID<0.53.0>) 1
   ```

How it works...

In step 1, we are using **errors** in a `try...rescue` block to capture a division by zero error:

```
def safe_division(a, b) do
  try do
    div(a,b)
  rescue
```

```
        _error -> _error
    end
  end
```

Normally, a division by zero generates this error:

iex(1)> div(9,0)

** (ArithmeticError) bad argument in arithmetic expression

   :erlang.div(9, 0)

By using `try...rescue`, we get a struct representing the `%ArithmeticError{}` error that we may use to gather/send information about what happened.

We could also specify the error message. Try replacing the `_error -> _error` line with `_error -> {:error, {:message, "division by zero error #{inspect(_error)}"}}`.

This would result in the following message whenever a division by zero is attempted:

`{:error, {:message, "division by zero error %ArithmeticError{}"}}`

In step 2, we are using **throws** with a `try...catch` block to capture a value for later usage:

```
  def throw_on_zero(list) do
    try do
      Enum.each list, fn(_number)->
        if _number == 0, do: throw(_number) end
      "Good! No zeros on the list!"
    catch
      _number -> "Oops! There was a #{_number} on the list!"
    end
  end
```

This construct should be used in those situations where we are not able to retrieve a value without the throw construct.

We start by traversing the list and if any of its elements is 0, we "throw" it to be handled in the `catch` block.

In step 3, we use **exits**. This kind of error mechanism is more suitable when dealing with processes. Every time a process dies, it sends a signal, which is an exit signal. In our example, we are actually spawning a function that outputs a message and terminates, passing the value 1 to the exit call:

```
  def shortest_living_process do
    IO.puts "Spawning process..."
    spawn_link fn ->
```

```
            IO.puts "Process started!"
          exit(1)
        end
    end
```

There's more...

The exit signals are quite important in the virtual machine. The supervisors receive these signals from their supervised processes, and this allows you to trigger the mechanisms defined in the supervising strategy.

As we have already seen, the use of the supervision tree is exactly what makes the use of this error handling construct uncommon.

Also, it's worth mentioning that in step 1, we are using the `try...rescue` block to capture any invalid input, in this case, 0. We are being defensive!

A possible approach would be to use a guard in the function definition to avoid even executing it if the input was "wrong", letting it crash!

Using a guard in the `safe_division` function would result in the following code:

```
def safe_division(a, b) when b != 0 do
  div(a,b)
end
```

The *Using guard clauses and pattern matching in function definitions* recipe in *Chapter 4, Modules and Functions*, has more information on this matter.

Packaging and releasing an OTP application

There comes a time when our supervision tree is wonderfully set up and our `gen_server` workers are ready to accept requests. Everything is fault-tolerant, concurrent, and ready to be distributed. Then, we have to actually create a release and start our code in different nodes.

In this recipe, we will be focusing on an Elixir library to help us with the release process: **exrm**.

Elixir Release Manager (exrm) defines its goal like this:

"This project's goal is to make releases with Elixir projects a breeze. It is composed of a mix task, and build files required to successfully take your Elixir project and perform a release build, and a simplified configuration mechanism which integrates with your current configuration and makes it easy for your operations group to configure the release once deployed."

Getting ready...

In this recipe, we will be releasing a Mix application that encapsulates our `ConnectionTracker` GenServer. You will find the code in the `release_me` directory.

To get ourselves started, we will add `exrm` to the dependencies of our project in our `mix.exs` file:

```
defp deps do
  [{:exrm, "~> 0.14.13"}]
end
```

Then, we will fetch the dependencies and compile them:

```
> mix deps.get
> mix deps.compile
```

How to do it...

To build a release for our project, we will follow these steps:

1. Compile your code:

    ```
    > mix compile
    Compiled lib/release_me.ex
    Compiled lib/ReleaseMe/connection_tracker.ex
    Generated release_me.app
    ```

2. Use the `mix release` task provided by exrm:

    ```
    > mix release
    ==> Building release with MIX_ENV=dev.
    ==> Generating relx configuration...
    ==> Generating sys.config...
    ==> Generating boot script...
    ==> Performing protocol consolidation...
    ==> Conform: Loading schema...
    ==> Conform: No schema found, conform will not be packaged in
        this release!
    ==> Generating release...
    ==> Generating nodetool...
    ==> Packaging release...
    ==> The release for release_me-0.0.1 is ready!
    ```

In some cases, when the `mix release` task is run for the first time, it may fail with a missing config file message. If this happens, please re-run the Mix task.

It's also worth mentioning that the directory where the application you wish to release is stored should not contain whitespaces in its path.

3. Run the app from the terminal, attaching it to an IEx console:

```
> rel/release_me/bin/release_me console
```

```
Exec: /Users/paulo/Desktop/release_me/rel/release_me/erts-6.2/
bin/erlexec -boot /Users/paulo/Desktop/release_me/rel/release_me/
releases/0.0.1/release_me -boot_var ERTS_LIB_DIR /Users/paulo/
Desktop/release_me/rel/release_me/erts-6.2/../lib -env ERL_LIBS
/Users/paulo/Desktop/release_me/rel/release_me/lib -config /
Users/paulo/Desktop/release_me/rel/release_me/releases/0.0.1/
sys.config -pa /Users/paulo/Desktop/release_me/rel/release_me/
lib/consolidated -args_file /Users/paulo/Desktop/release_me/rel/
release_me/releases/0.0.1/vm.args -user Elixir.IEx.CLI -extra
--no-halt +iex -- console
```

```
Root: /Users/paulo/Desktop/release_me/rel/release_me
```

```
/Users/paulo/Desktop/release_me/rel/release_me
```

```
Erlang/OTP 17 [erts-6.2] [source] [64-bit] [smp:8:8] [async-
threads:10] [hipe] [kernel-poll:false] [dtrace]
```

```
Interactive Elixir (1.0.2) - press Ctrl+C to exit (type h() ENTER
for help)
```

```
iex(release_me@127.0.0.1)1>
```

4. Start the server and make some requests:

```
iex(release_me@127.0.0.1)1> {:ok, pid} = ReleaseMe.
ConnectionTracker.start_link
```

```
{:ok, #PID<0.79.0>}
```

```
iex(release_me@127.0.0.1)2> ReleaseMe.ConnectionTracker.add_
user(pid, {:test, "demo"})
```

```
:ok
```

```
iex(release_me@127.0.0.1)3> ReleaseMe.ConnectionTracker.search_
user(pid, :test)
```

```
{:ok, "demo"}
```

In step 3, we executed the application with the console argument. This automatically attaches a console session to the running application. If we wished, we could have started the application with the following command:

```
> rel/release_me/bin/release_me start
```

This would actually start the application. If we wished to attach a console to the running node later, we could use this command:

```
> rel/release_me/bin/release_me attach
```

This would provide us with this output:

```
Attaching to /tmp/erl_pipes/release_me/erlang.pipe.1 (^D
to exit)

iex(release_me@127.0.0.1)1>
```

The console is now ready and allows interaction with the system.

How it works...

In step 1, when we performed the compilation, a `.app` file was generated with the information needed to build our application and make it self-contained.

In step 2, we actually built the application. If you take a look at the `rel` directory, you will find all the files needed to run the application.

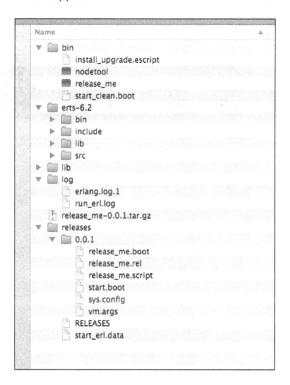

The executable we used in step 3 is located inside the `bin` folder.

This recipe emphasizes one of the biggest strengths of Elixir: **tooling**.

With a few simple commands, we were able to build and package a self-contained OTP application that is ready to be deployed!

If you wonder why there is a `releases/0.0.1` folder, check the `mix.exs` file. In the `project` section, the version is defined as `0.0.1`.

If we wish to upgrade and enhance our application and build a new release, we just have to implement the features, update the version number, and generate the release again. This allows for the existence of different versions of applications and it is even possible to upgrade/downgrade running applications without stopping them!

There's more...

exrm has some interesting features and can be used with **conform** (`https://github.com/bitwalker/conform`) to adapt the application to its deployed environment.

See also

▶ In the *Deploying applications and updating a running system* recipe, we will look at how to use exrm to help us with deployments and how to manage versions in running systems

Deploying applications and updating a running system

In this recipe, we will be using exrm to assist us in the process of deploying applications and updating running systems without taking them down.

This is another key feature provided by Elixir: **availability**!

Getting ready

To get started, we need the application that we used in the previous recipe. You may find it under the `release_me` folder in the code directory.

How to do it...

To deploy an application and update it while running, we will follow these steps:

1. Create a new location to deploy your application. In this case, we will be using the `tmp/elixir_app` directory:

   ```
   mkdir -p tmp/elixir_app
   ```

2. Copy the release generated in the previous recipe to the new location:

   ```
   > cp rel/release_me/release_me-0.0.1.tar.gz tmp/elixir_app
   ```

3. Unpack it:

   ```
   > cd tmp/elixir_app
   > tar -xf release_me-0.0.1.tar.gz
   ```

4. Start your app by running the following command after going to the root directory of your application, that is, the rel/release_me folder:

   ```
   > bin/release_me start
   ```

5. To upgrade your application, generate a new release, following the instructions from the previous recipe.

 Don't forget to update the version number in the `mix.exs` file!

6. Once you have the `release_me-0.0.2.tar.gz` file, follow steps 2 and 3.

7. To actually update the code while it is running, use this command:

   ```
   > bin/release_me upgrade "0.0.2"
   ```

How it works...

The release tool exrm hides away most of the complexity related to building, deploying, and upgrading systems. It's a great help to every Elixir developer and is one of the examples of brilliant tooling and the amazing community of Elixir.

 Code upgrading relies on the implementation of the `code_change()` callback in the upgradable modules.

See also

▸   For a deeper understanding of the release mechanisms, the documentation at
    `http://www.erlang.org/doc/system_principles/system_principles.`
    `html` is really helpful.

7

Cowboy and Phoenix

This chapter will cover the following recipes:

- ▶ Cowboy
    - ❑ Setting up Cowboy
    - ❑ Serving static files
    - ❑ Implementing a websocket handler
- ▶ Phoenix
    - ❑ Creating a Phoenix application
    - ❑ Defining routes
    - ❑ Creating a controller
    - ❑ Creating views and templates
    - ❑ Implementing topics
    - ❑ Protecting the Phoenix app with SSL

Introduction

In this chapter, we will look at **Cowboy** and **Phoenix**.

Cowboy is written in Erlang and its author, Loïc Hoguin, defines it as "a small, fast, and modular HTTP server."

Cowboy provides an HTTP 1.0/1.1 stack and supports websockets, SPDY, and REST. It is currently used in Phoenix, which is an Elixir web framework.

Phoenix was a project started by Chris McCord but currently has several contributors and is an excellent option to implement web applications. Its aim is to provide a way to build full-featured, fault tolerant applications with real-time functionalities.

We will begin by showing you how to use Cowboy. Even though it is written in Erlang, its use with Elixir is possible and is proof of the excellent interoperability between Elixir and Erlang.

Later on, we will use Phoenix to create a simple web application.

Setting up Cowboy

In this recipe, we will set up Cowboy. We will add it as a dependency for our application and get ready to implement some functionalities, such as static file serving and websockets, in later recipes.

Getting ready

To get ourselves started, we will create a Mix application. To do this, enter the following command in a terminal window:

```
> mix new cowboy_app --sup
```

How to do it...

Now that we have created our Elixir application, we will set up Cowboy by following these steps:

1. Add Cowboy as a dependency in the `mix.exs` file under the `deps` method:

   ```
   defp deps do
     [
       { :cowboy, "~> 1.0.0"}
     ]
   end
   ```

2. Fetch the dependencies by issuing the following command in a terminal window:

   ```
   > mix deps.get
   ```

The dependencies will be fetched and the output will be similar to this:

```
→ cowboy_app  mix deps.get
Dependency resolution completed successfully
* Getting cowboy (Hex package)
Checking package (https://s3.amazonaws.com/s3.hex.pm/tarballs/cowboy-1.0.0.tar)
Fetched package
Unpacked package tarball (/Users/paulo/.hex/packages/cowboy-1.0.0.tar)
* Getting cowlib (Hex package)
Checking package (https://s3.amazonaws.com/s3.hex.pm/tarballs/cowlib-1.0.1.tar)
Fetched package
Unpacked package tarball (/Users/paulo/.hex/packages/cowlib-1.0.1.tar)
* Getting ranch (Hex package)
Checking package (https://s3.amazonaws.com/s3.hex.pm/tarballs/ranch-1.0.0.tar)
Fetched package
Unpacked package tarball (/Users/paulo/.hex/packages/ranch-1.0.0.tar)
→ cowboy_app
```

Dependencies' installation

3. We will now compile the dependencies:

   ```
   > mix deps.compile
   ```

4. Before we can use Cowboy, there is still one thing to do. We will add it to the `applications` section in our `mix.exs` file:

   ```
   def application do
     [applications: [:logger, :cowboy],
      mod: {Chapter7, []}]
   end
   ```

5. To make sure everything is working, we will start our application inside an IEx session:

   ```
   > iex -S mix
   ```

6. Now, inside our IEx session, we will check whether Cowboy was started and is ready to be used by querying our currently running applications:

   ```
   iex(1)> :application.which_applications
   [{:cowboy_app, 'cowboy_app', '0.0.1'},
    {:cowboy, 'Small, fast, modular HTTP server.', '1.0.0'},
    {:cowlib, 'Support library for manipulating Web protocols.',
   '1.0.1'},
   ```

```
{:ranch, 'Socket acceptor pool for TCP protocols.', '1.0.0'},
{:logger, 'logger', '1.0.2'}, {:inets, 'INETS  CXC 138 49',
'5.10.4'},
{:ssl, 'Erlang/OTP SSL application', '5.3.8'},
{:public_key, 'Public key infrastructure', '0.22.1'},
{:asn1, 'The Erlang ASN1 compiler version 3.0.3', '3.0.3'},
{:mix, 'mix', '1.0.2'}, {:iex, 'iex', '1.0.2'}, {:elixir,
'elixir', '1.0.2'},
{:syntax_tools, 'Syntax tools', '1.6.17'},
{:compiler, 'ERTS  CXC 138 10', '5.0.3'}, {:crypto, 'CRYPTO',
'3.4.2'},
{:stdlib, 'ERTS  CXC 138 10', '2.3'}, {:kernel, 'ERTS  CXC 138
10', '3.1'}]
```

How it works...

In step 1, we add Cowboy as a dependency in our application. The dependency management in Mix applications is covered in the *Managing dependencies* recipe of *Chapter 1, Command Line*.

Here, even though Cowboy is an Erlang application, we use the package available via the Hex package manager (https://hex.pm/packages/cowboy).

> If we wished, we could have also used the Git repository for Cowboy as the source for our dependency. It would just be a matter of replacing [{:cowboy, "~> 1.0.0"}] with [{:cowboy, git: "git://github.com/ninenines/cowboy"}}].

In step 2, we fetch the dependencies and we compile them in step 3.

Cowboy has two associated dependencies: ranch and cowlib. They are, respectively, a socket acceptor pool for TCP protocols and support library to manipulate web protocols.

Afterwards, in step 4, we add Cowboy to the list of applications to be started. This ensures that when we initialize our Mix application, Cowboy and its dependencies will also be running, ready to perform their tasks. We checked this by starting the application (step 5) and making sure they were part of the running applications (step 6).

The result of the command contains Cowboy, cowlib, and ranch on the list of running applications, so everything is properly set up and ready for use!

There's more...

Now that we have successfully configured Cowboy, it's time to use it to implement some features in our Mix application!

- ▶ We will use Cowboy as a static file server in the *Serving static files* recipe
- ▶ We also use Cowboy to establish websocket connections and allow bi-directional communication between servers and clients in the *Implementing a websocket handler* recipe

Serving static files

In this recipe, we will take our configured Cowboy application and add the ability to serve static files requested via HTTP.

Getting ready

We will start by opening the source files in the `Code/Chapter 7/cowboy_static/cowboy_app` folder in our favorite editor.

How to do it...

To add the ability to serve static files to our application, follow these steps:

1. Create a new folder inside the `lib` directory and name it `cowboy`.
2. Inside this new folder, create a file named `root_page_handler.ex`.
3. Add the following code to the file:

`cowboy_app/lib/root_page_handler.ex`

```
defmodule Cowboy.RootPageHandler do
  def init(_transport, req, []) do
    {:ok, req, nil}
  end

  def handle(req, state) do
    {:ok, req} = :cowboy_req.chunked_reply(200, req)
    :ok = :cowboy_req.chunk("Root page text rendered by the
handler. No file defining this content!\r\n", req)
    {:ok, req, state}
  end

  def terminate(_reason, _req, _state), do: :ok
end
```

4. Inside this same folder, create a file called `dispatch.ex`.

5. Add this code to define the `dispatch` module:

```
cowboy_app/lib/dispatch.ex

defmodule Cowboy.Dispatch do
  def start do

    dispatch = :cowboy_router.compile([
      { :_,
        [
          {"/", Cowboy.RootPageHandler, []},
          {"/[...]", :cowboy_static, { :priv_dir, :cowboy_app,
"", [{:mimetypes, :cow_mimetypes, :all}]}}
        ]
      }
    ])
    {:ok, _} = :cowboy.start_http(:cowboy_app, 100, [{:port,
8080}], [{:env, [{:dispatch, dispatch}]}])

  end

end
```

6. Now let's edit the `lib/cowboy_app.ex` file and add the call to the method that will initialize our defined dispatch. Place the following highlighted code right after the `import Supervisor.Spec, warn: false` line:

```
defmodule CowboyApp do
  use Application

  def start(_type, _args) do
    import Supervisor.Spec, warn: false

    Cowboy.Dispatch.start

    children = [
      # Define workers and child supervisors to be supervised
      # worker(CowboyApp.Worker, [arg1, arg2, arg3])
    ]

    opts = [strategy: :one_for_one, name: CowboyApp.Supervisor]
    Supervisor.start_link(children, opts)
  end
end
```

Cowboy provides its own supervisor. This is why we don't place it under our app's supervision tree.

7. Start the Mix application:

   ```
   > iex -S mix
   ```

8. Visit the root page (`http://localhost:8080/`):

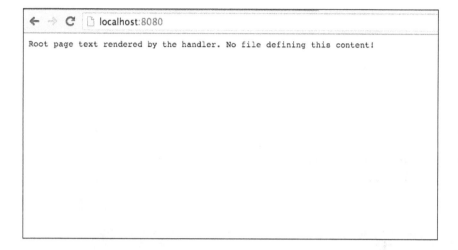

9. Visit the `index.html` sample page at `http://localhost:8080/index.html`:

10. Visit the `test.html` sample page at `http://localhost:8080/test.html`:

11. Now let's open some images, as shown in this screenshot (`http://localhost:8080/html.jpg`):

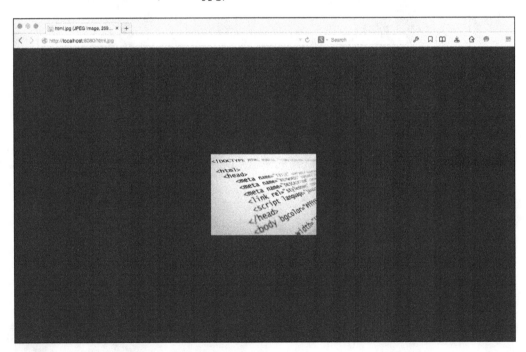

This is another image downloaded from `http://localhost:8080/cc.png`:

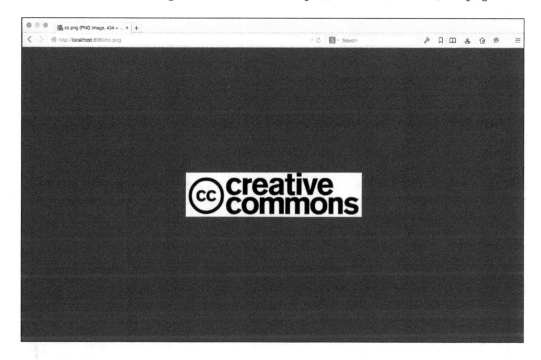

How it works...

In step 1, we defined a namespace for our modules by creating the `cowboy` folder. As you can see, the files we created in this recipe have `Cowboy` prepended.

> We could have used any other name. There is no need to create a Cowboy namespace to implement any of these features!

In steps 2 and 3, we implement a module that will respond to any requests made to the root path of our server. The `Cowboy.RootPageHandler` module has two methods: `init` and `handle`. It is inside the latter that we define the desired behavior. In this case, we define the text that should be rendered in the client browser. Although this is not actually a static file, it is included to showcase the implementation of a generic handler with Cowboy. The result of a request to this resource is exemplified in step 8.

In steps 4 and 5, we define the `Cowboy.Dispatch` module. This module's responsibility is to determine, given the request, what should be handled and how.

We start by defining that the root path, / will be handled by the `Cowboy.RootPageHandler` module as `{"/", Cowboy.RootPageHandler, []}`.

Then we define the handler for any other file (/ [...]):

```
{"/[...]", :cowboy_static, { :priv_dir, :cowboy_app,
"", [{:mimetypes,:cow_mimetypes,:all}]}}
```

The directory we define as the source for the static files is `priv`. By default, the `:priv_dir` atom refers to the `priv` directory inside the application with the name defined by the next atom (in this case, `:cowboy_app`). If you look inside it, you will find the HTML and image files we requested in steps 9 and 10 there. The `:cowboy_static` atom refers to a module implemented by Cowboy that serves static files. The reason we don't need to define it is because that is already taken care for us. In this line, we also register the mime types we wish to handle. One of Cowboys dependencies, cowlib, allows us to do so with the `{:mimetypes,:cow_mimetypes,:all}` tuple.

We could resume the line that registers the static handle in the following way:

For every request to `/foo.bar`, use the `cowboy_static` module and look for the `foo.bar` file with the `bar` mime type inside the `priv` dir of `cowboy_app`.

 If we switch the order of the lines defining the root page handler and the static files, the root page handler will never be triggered, as / [...] will always match first!

In this case, when `http://localhost:8080/` is requested, the result is a blank page!

Implementing a websocket handler

In this recipe, we will add a websocket handler to our Cowboy application. We will also change the index page to allow us to send messages. The index page will continue to be served by the static handler we defined previously. With websockets enabled, all clients connected to `index.html` will receive the messages sent by other clients without the need to refresh the page.

Getting ready

We will iterate over the code used in the previous recipe. A copy of the finished code can be found in the `Code/Chapter 7/cowboy_websockets/cowboy_app` directory.

To get started, we will load the code in our code editor.

The code is almost the same as the one used in the previous recipe with some changes to `priv/index.html` and some CSS, JavaScript, and fonts added.

How to do it...

To add websockets support to our Cowboy application, follow these steps:

1. Define a handler for websockets in the `lib/cowboy/ws_handler.ex` file:

```elixir
defmodule Cowboy.WsHandler do
  @behaviour :cowboy_websocket_handler

  def init({:tcp, :http}, _req, _opts) do
    {:upgrade, :protocol, :cowboy_websocket}
  end

  def websocket_init(_transport_name, req, _opts) do
    Cowboy.WsServer.join(self())
    {:ok, req, :undefinded_state}
  end

  def websocket_handle({:text, msg}, req, state) do
    # change :others to all if you wish to notify the sender too!
    Cowboy.WsServer.send_messages(:others, self(), msg)
    {:ok, req, state}
  end
  def websocket_handle(_data, req, state) do
    {:ok, req, state}
  end

  def websocket_info({:send_message, _server_pid, msg}, req, state) do
    {:reply, {:text, msg}, req, state}
  end
  def websocket_info(_info, req, state) do
    {:ok, req, state}
  end

  def websocket_terminate(_reason, _req, _state) do
    Cowboy.WsServer.leave(self())
    :ok
  end
end
```

2. Register the handler in the dispatch (`cowboy/dispatch.ex`) by adding the following line right below the root handler:

```elixir
{"/websocket", Cowboy.WsHandler, []},
```

3. Create a GenServer (`lib/cowboy/ws_server.ex`) that will be called by the websocket handler to send messages and hold a list of connected clients:

```
defmodule Cowboy.WsServer do
  use GenServer
  require Record
  Record.defrecord :state, [clients: []]

  ### client API
  def start_link(opts \\ []) do
    :gen_server.start_link({:local, __MODULE__}, __MODULE__, :ok,
opts)
  end

  def join(pid) do
    :gen_server.cast(__MODULE__, {:join, pid})
  end

  def leave(pid) do
    :gen_server.cast(__MODULE__, {:leave, pid})
  end

  def send_messages(:others, pid, message) do
    :gen_server.cast(__MODULE__, {:send_message, pid, message})
  end

  def send_messages(:all, pid, message) do
    :gen_server.cast(__MODULE__, {:notify_all, pid, message})
  end

  ### server Callbacks
  def init(:ok) do
    state = state()
    {:ok, state}
  end

  def handle_cast({:join, pid}, state) do
    current_clients = state(state, :clients)
    all_clients = [pid|current_clients]
    new_state = state(clients: all_clients)
    {:noreply, new_state}
  end
  def handle_cast({:leave, pid}, state) do
    all_clients = state(state, :clients)
    others = all_clients -- [pid]
```

```
      new_state = state(clients: others)
      {:noreply, new_state}
    end
    def handle_cast({:send_message, pid, message}, state) do
      send_message(:others, pid, message, state)
      {:noreply, state}
    end
    def handle_cast({:notify_all, pid, message}, state) do
      send_message(:all, pid, message, state)
      {:noreply, state}
    end

    def handle_info(_info, state) do
      {:noreply, state}
    end

    def terminate(_reason, _state) do
      :ok
    end

    ### internal funs
    defp send_message(:others, pid, message, state) do
      clients = state(state, :clients)
      others = clients -- [pid]
      Enum.each(others, &(send(&1,{:send_message, self(),
message}})))
    end
    defp send_message(:all, _pid, message, state) do
      clients = state(state, :clients)
      Enum.each(clients, &(send(&1,{:send_message, self(),
message}})))
    end
end
```

4. Register the GenServer under the supervision tree by adding the following code to `cowboy_app.ex`:

```
children = [
  worker(Cowboy.WsServer, [])
]
```

5. Start the application:

    ```
    > iex -S mix
    ```

6. Open two different browser windows, visit `http://localhost:8080/index.html` and start sending messages between them.

How it works...

To implement a websocket handler, apart from adding some JS, CSS files, and fonts and editing the index page to create a interface to start messaging between browsers, we need to create a GenServer and a Cowboy handler for websockets. Let's take a closer look at how we achieved our goal.

In step 1, we begin by defining a websocket handler. The second line of the `ws_handler.ex` file has an annotation that defines a behavior: `@behaviour :cowboy_websocket_handler`. This defines the interface for a websocket handler and forces us to define several functions in the file to comply with that behavior.

 For more information about the `@behaviour` annotation, refer to the *Enforcing behaviors* recipe in *Chapter 4, Modules and Functions*.

The functions defined are `init`, `websocket_init`, `websocket_handle`, `websocket_info`, and `websocket_terminate`.

We will now see each of these functions in more detail:

- `init`: This function is responsible for the upgrade of the protocol to `cowboy_websocket`.

- `websocket_init`: This function is called before the actual protocol upgrade occurs and is where any state is initialized normally. In this particular case, we perform a call to the `join` function of the `ws_server.ex` GenServer we chose to implement. There, we add the PID of the new connected client to a list of all connected clients (the `ws_server.ex` file's lines 11-13 and 37-42).

- `websocket_handle`: This function handles the data received via the websocket. We defined two versions of this function. The first one deals with the case of messages with the `{:text, msg}` format and the other deals with any other type of websocket messages. We used pattern matching, so the only time we actually perform any action is when a message arrives in the `{:text, msg}` format. We call the `ws_server.ex` GenServer function to send messages to all clients except the one sending the message. If you wish to change this behavior, change the `:others` atom to `:all` in line 16 of the `ws_handler.ex` file. The lines of the GenServer that deal with this are 49-56 and 71-79.

- `websocket_info`: This function is responsible for handling any non-websocket messages received. Similar to the `websocket_handle` function, we defined two versions of this function: the first one to respond to the received messages with the `{:send_message, _server_pid, msg}` format and the last one to handle any other type of non-websocket messages. It is here that we actually perform the sending of the message to the client.

▶ `websocket_terminate`: This is the function responsible for performing any cleanup tasks when the websocket connection is closed. In our code, we invoke the `ws_server.ex` file's `Cowboy.WsServer.leave` function, passing the PID of the handler process (`self()`). This function unregisters this process from the list of connected clients maintained in the GenServer.

In step 2, we register the handler on the Cowboy dispatch. This is a way to define that any requests established via the `ws://` protocol to the websockets endpoint will be handled by this handler.

 In the `cowboy_websockets/cowboy_app/priv/js/index.js` file's lines 19 and 20, we define the connection to `ws://localhost:8080/websockets`.

Steps 3 and 4 are where we define the GenServer associated with the websocket handler and then start it under the application supervisor.

 We will not go into details of the GenServer implementation. More details on GenServer can be found in the *Implementing a GenServer* and *Expanding our server* recipes in *Chapter 6, OTP – Open Telecom Platform*.

In steps 5 and 6, we start using the websocket support to send messages that appear in real time on all connected browsers.

There's more...

For browsers that do not support websockets, there is an alternative named **Bullet**, also created by Cowboy's author, Loïc Hoguin. It consists of an Erlang application and a JavaScript library (`bullet.js`) that provides a compatibility layer via fallback mechanisms such as long-poling to browsers that don't support websockets. More information can be found at `https://github.com/extend/bullet`.

We have included it and used it in this recipe in order to make it work in as many browsers as possible.

Creating a Phoenix application

The following recipes of this chapter will relate to an Elixir web framework: Phoenix.

Phoenix is an implementation of the server-side MVC pattern. It is very similar to Ruby on Rails or Python Django, but it is much more than a mere clone.

Phoenix's goal is to combine the high productivity of the mentioned frameworks with high performance, and introduces several concepts such as **channels** for websocket management, **topics** as a pub-sub layer, and precompiled **templates** as well.

Chris McCord created Phoenix, and the first commit dates from May 1, 2014. The implementation pace is impressive and it currently has almost all of the features defined in the initial roadmap; only iOS and Android clients are pending. This project now has more than 80 committers and among them is José Valim, the creator of Elixir.

Our first recipe on Phoenix will show you how to create an application. We will generate the canonical to-do application.

Getting ready

To get started with Phoenix and create a new application, we will need to clone the `phoenixframework` repository from GitHub. Open a terminal window and go to the directory where you want to place Phoenix.

Start by cloning the repository with the following command:

```
> git clone https://github.com/phoenixframework/phoenix.git
```

Go to the `phoenix` directory and check out the `<x.y.z>` version:

```
> cd phoenix && git checkout v0.8.0
```

Get the dependencies and compile `phoenix`:

```
> mix do deps.get, compile
```

How to do it...

To create a new Phoenix application, follow these steps:

1. Generate the application from the cloned `phoenix` directory:

   ```
   > mix phoenix.new todo ../todo
   ```

2. Go to the generated application directory:

   ```
   > cd ../todo
   ```

3. Install and compile the application dependencies:

   ```
   > mix do deps.get, compile
   ```

4. Test everything by starting the server:

   ```
   > mix phoenix.server
   Running Todo.Endpoint with Cowboy on port 4000 (http)
   ```

5. Open a browser window and visit `http://localhost:4000`, as shown in the following screenshot:

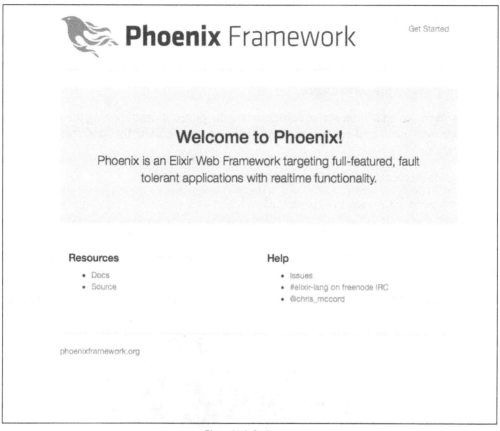

Phoenix default page

How it works...

The Phoenix application we have cloned defines several Mix tasks. For more information on the creation of custom Mix tasks, refer to the *Creating custom Mix tasks* recipe in *Chapter 1, Command Line*.

One of these tasks, `phoenix.new`, is responsible for generating the structure of a Phoenix application, taking into account the name of the app and the location where you want to create it. These were the two parameters we passed to the task in step 1.

Afterwards, the procedure is pretty much standard in what is related to Mix applications: get the dependencies, compile, and start the application. In the particular case of Phoenix, as we saw in step 4, there is also a Mix task that starts the application (`mix phoenix.server`).

There's more...

In the introduction to this recipe, I mentioned one of the goals of Phoenix: associate high productivity with high performance.

In the following recipes, we will be focusing on some common tasks that can give you an idea of the productivity gains with this framework.

Now we will focus on the performance.

We will perform two additional steps, consolidating the protocols and running the application in the production mode by disabling features such as code reloading that definitely slow down our application.

To consolidate protocols, use the following command:

```
> MIX_ENV=prod mix compile.protocols
```

Now, to start the application in the production mode, use the following command:

```
> MIX_ENV=prod PORT=4001 elixir -pa _build/prod/consolidated -S mix
phoenix.start
```

It's time to test the application with the **wrk** tool; performing 15 concurrent requests with 15 connections in 1 minute, we get these results:

```
→  ~  wrk -c15 -t15 -d60s http://localhost:4001
Running 1m test @ http://localhost:4001
  15 threads and 15 connections
  Thread Stats   Avg      Stdev     Max    +/- Stdev
    Latency     4.62ms    4.43ms   61.92ms   95.28%
    Req/Sec   263.95     81.33     1.00k    69.07%
  227442 requests in 1.00m, 453.97MB read
Requests/sec:   3793.01
Transfer/sec:      7.57MB
→  ~
```

The machine used to run the Phoenix web app was my laptop, a 2011 MacBook Pro 13' (2.3 GHz Intel Core i5), and even with this machine, Phoenix was able to serve 3,793 requests per second!

Defining routes

In the previous recipe, we created our first Phoenix application. In this recipe, we will add some routes to the phoenix to-do application.

By adding routes, we define the behavior of the application whenever a given URL/endpoint is accessed. The `Router` task is used to parse the requests and then dispatch them to the current controller's action, passing any existing parameters to it.

Getting ready

Open the file generated in the previous recipe in your code editor. A copy of the full code for this recipe can be found at `Code/Chapter 7/phoenix_routes/todo/web/router.ex`:

```
defmodule Todo.Router do
  use Phoenix.Router

  pipeline :browser do
    plug :accepts, ~w(html)
    plug :fetch_session
    plug :fetch_flash
    plug :protect_from_forgery
  end

  pipeline :api do
    plug :accepts, ~w(json)
  end

  scope "/", Todo do
    pipe_through :browser # Use the default browser stack

    get "/", PageController, :index

    get "/text", MyController, :plaintext
    get "/generated", MyController, :send_html

  end

  # Other scopes may use custom stacks.
  # scope "/api", Todo do
  #   pipe_through :api
  # end
end
```

How to do it...

To define some routes, follow these steps:

1. Add the routes to define the `/text` and `/generated` endpoints. Below `get "/"`, `PageController, :index`, add these two lines:

   ```
   get "/text", MyController, :plaintext
   get "/generated", MyController, :send_html
   ```

2. Define the routes to a resource by adding `resources "todos",`
    `TodosController` to the `router.ex` file:

```
defmodule Todo.Router do
  use Phoenix.Router

  pipeline :browser do
    plug :accepts, ~w(html)
    plug :fetch_session
    plug :fetch_flash
    plug :protect_from_forgery
  end

  pipeline :api do
    plug :accepts, ~w(json)
  end

  scope "/", Todo do
    pipe_through :browser # Use the default browser stack

    get "/", PageController, :index

    get "/text", MyController, :plaintext
    get "/generated", MyController, :send_html

    resources "todos", TodosController

  end

  # Other scopes may use custom stacks.
  # scope "/api", Todo do
  #   pipe_through :api
  # end
end
```

How it works...

As mentioned in the introduction to this recipe, the router is responsible for parsing incoming requests and dispatching them to the controller action that will handle the request.

In step 1, we defined how requests to `/text` and `/generated` will be handled.

The generic definition is `<method_macro> <path>, <controller>, <action>`. We use the `get` macro in both examples in step 1. This elixir macro expands and corresponds to the HTTP `GET` verb. There are macros defined for the other verbs (`PUT`, `POST`, `PATCH`, `DELETE`, `HEAD`, `OPTIONS`, `CONNECT` and `TRACE`).

The macro takes three arguments. The `<path>` argument is the endpoint we wish to define. The `<controller>` and `<action>` arguments specify the module and function responsible for handling the request.

In step 2, we defined a route using the `resource` macro. This macro only takes two arguments: the name of the resource and the controller that will handle requests related to that resource. When we use this macro, we will get eight actual endpoints for the `todo` resource:

```
todos_path   GET     /todos            Todo.TodosController.index/2
todos_path   GET     /todos/:id/edit   Todo.TodosController.edit/2
todos_path   GET     /todos/new        Todo.TodosController.new/2
todos_path   GET     /todos/:id        Todo.TodosController.show/2
todos_path   POST    /todos            Todo.TodosController.create/2
todos_path   PATCH   /todos/:id        Todo.TodosController.update/2
             PUT     /todos/:id        Todo.TodosController.update/2
todos_path   DELETE  /todos/:id        Todo.TodosController.destroy/2
```

We will have to implement the `index/2`, `edit/2`, `new/2`, `show/2`, `create/2`, `update/2` and `destroy/2` functions (or actions, as they are called in this context) in the `TodosController` module (in this context, the controller).

There's more...

When defining a route using the `resources` macro, it is possible to define which actions to include or exclude.

We will look into two examples about the usage of the `resources` macro with the `only` and `except` directives.

First, define that our `todo` resources will only be listed and viewed (`index` and `show` actions):

```
resources "todos", TodosController, only: [:index, :show]
```

 The actions referred here are functions defined in the controller. Some actions are standard in REST. For more information on REST, please visit `http://restful-api-design.readthedocs.org/en/latest/methods.html`.

Then define that our `todo` resources may not be changed after being created (no editing will be possible):

```
resources "todos", TodosController, except: [:edit, :update]
```

To inspect the routes generated by each of these options, run `mix phoenix.routes` in the command line inside the application's root directory.

See also

▶ For more information on the router, visit `http://www.phoenixframework.org/v0.8.0/docs/routing`

Creating a controller

In Phoenix, controllers are Elixir modules that define functions (or actions) to handle the requests dispatched by the router. The controllers are responsible for preparing and passing data to the view layer and determining the rendering of these views.

Getting ready

To get started, we will extend the project defined in the *Defining routes* recipe. The defined routes are as follows:

```
page_path   GET      /                    Todo.PageController.index/2
  my_path   GET      /text                Todo.MyController.plaintext/2
  my_path   GET      /generated           Todo.MyController.send_html/2
todos_path  GET      /todos               Todo.TodosController.index/2
todos_path  GET      /todos/:id/edit      Todo.TodosController.edit/2
todos_path  GET      /todos/new           Todo.TodosController.new/2
todos_path  GET      /todos/:id           Todo.TodosController.show/2
todos_path  POST     /todos               Todo.TodosController.create/2
todos_path  PATCH    /todos/:id           Todo.TodosController.update/2
            PUT      /todos/:id           Todo.TodosController.update/2
todos_path  DELETE   /todos/:id           Todo.TodosController.destroy/2
```

The root path (`page_path`) is handled by the `PageController` controller. This controller was generated by default with the application. We will need to create the controllers to handle the entries under `my_path` and `todos_path`. To do this, will create two new files: `todo/web/controllers/my_controller.ex` and `todo/web/controllers/todos_controller.ex`.

How to do it...

To create a controller, follow these steps:

1. We will start by adding the action that will handle requests to the `/text` endpoint. Inside `my_controller.ex`, add the following code:

```
defmodule Todo.MyController do
  use Phoenix.Controller

  plug :action

  def plaintext(conn, _params) do
    text conn, "Plain text rendered from Phoenix controller!"
  end

end
```

2. Now we will add an action to handle requests performed to the `generated` endpoint by adding this code right below the plaintext action defined in the previous step:

```
def send_html(conn, _params) do
  generated = """
    <html>
      <head>
        <title>Generated HTML</title>
      </head>
      <body>
        <h2>Creating Controllers</h2>
        <p>It is possible to render html from a Phoenix
controller!</p>
      </body>
    </html>
    """

  html conn, generated
end
```

3. Now we will define the index action (that lists all `todos`) for the `todos` resource. We will define it inside the `todos_controller` module:

```
defmodule Todo.TodosController do
  use Phoenix.Controller

  plug :action

  def index(conn, _params) do
```

```
      todo = [%{id: 1, task: "Write the other controller actions!",
created_at: "2014-12-13", status: "pending"}, %{id: 2, task:
"Create Views", created_at: "2014-12-13", status: "pending"}]
      json conn, todo
    end
  end
```

> To make this recipe more compact, we will change the line that defines the routes for the todos resource. Open the router file (web/router.ex) and find the following line:
>
> ```
> resources "todos", TodosController
> ```
>
> Change it to this:
>
> ```
> resources "todos", TodosController, only: [:index]
> ```
>
> This way, only the index action needs to be defined in order to have a working controller.

4. Now it's time to start the server (mix phoenix.server) and visit all the endpoints for which we have defined controller actions to check the result of our work:

    1. http://localhost:4000/text

    2. http://localhost:4000/generated

    3. http://localhost:4000/todos

How it works...

Both controllers we defined are "namespaced" with the application name (Todo), and both import the Phoenix.Controller module. This way, they have access to functions made available by that module (more information on this mechanism is available in *Using module directives* recipe in *Chapter 4, Modules and Functions*). The controllers also share the plug :action line. This is a macro that handles dispatching to the right controller and action according to what is defined in the router.

All of the functions, or actions, defined also share a common pattern: arguments.

They all accept conn and _params. The first argument is the structure that represents the connection, and following Elixir's message-passing, non-state sharing philosophy, the connection is received as an argument and then returned as part of the result. In all three cases, we return the connection:

▶ text **conn** "Plain text rendered from Phoenix controller!"

▶ json **conn** todos

▶ html **conn** generated

In the three controller actions we defined, we have used the text, HTML, and JSON macros.

They define the type of data we will send as response.

There's more...

In step 3, we define the `todos` list as a structure (map) inside the controller. Phoenix supports the interaction with the data stored in databases. You can use ETS, DETS, and Mnesia, and you can also use an external database, such as PostgreSQL, via an Elixir project named Ecto. To know more about this, please visit Ecto project's website (`http://github.com/elixir-lang/ecto`).

Creating views and templates

After the router determines the right controller and action to handle a request after the controller performs all the tasks to prepare data to respond to the request, it generally needs to output that data. In the previous recipe, we saw how a controller could respond by rendering test and outputting static HTML or even JSON. What if we need to generate an HTML response and that HTML must be dynamic, depending on the values passed by the controller?

Before we proceed, there is one thing we have to make clear for those coming from other frameworks: the view is not an HTML (or other markup) file. Views mainly render templates but they are also responsible for providing functions that make data easier to consume by templates. In Phoenix, a view is more like a decorator.

We may also use templates and layouts. Templates are the HTML structure where data obtained via the controller and prepared by the view is displayed. Layouts are a way to define a common structure shared by (possibly) multiple templates.

In this recipe, we will change the response of the `TodosController` index action. Instead of returning JSON containing the `todos`, we will output the data in an HTML page.

Getting ready

To get started, open the application resulting from the *Creating a controller* recipe and find this line:

```
json conn, todos
```

Replace it with this line:

```
assign(conn, :todos, todos)
```

We will also add `plug :render` right below `plug :action`.

The file should look like this:

```
defmodule Todo.TodosController do
  use Phoenix.Controller

  plug :action
  plug :render

  def index(conn, _params) do
    todos = [%{id: 1, task: "Write the other controller actions!",
created_at: "2014-12-13", status: "pending"}, %{id: 2, task: "Create
Views", created_at: "2014-12-13", status: "pending"}]
    assign(conn, :todos, todos)
  end
end
```

How to do it...

After changing the controller so that it renders a view, we will follow these steps to create the view and a new layout:

1. Create a view by adding a new `web/views/todos.view.ex` file with the following content:

```
defmodule Todo.TodosView do
  use Todo.View
  def todos(conn) do
    Enum.map(conn.assigns.todos, fn(x)->x[:task] end)
  end
end
```

2. Create a new template by adding the templates' `/todos/index.html.eex` file with this markup:

```
<div>
 <h3>Views and Templates</h3>
   <p>This is the template that will display only the task
     for each item in our todo list.</p>
   <ol>
     <p>TODO:</p>
     <%= for t <- todos @conn do %>
       <li><%= t %></li>
     <% end %>
   </ol>
 </div>
```

3. Start the Phoenix application:

```
> mix phoenix.server
```

4. Visit `http://localhost:4000/todos` to see the new template render a list with pending tasks.

How it works...

In step 1, we define our view. As was mentioned in the introduction to the recipe, the view acts like a decorator. In the index action of `TodosController`, we pass a structure and a list of maps, each one defining a `todo` map. These maps have several keys: `id`, `task`, `created_at`, and `status`. We use the view to filter each of the elements of the list and get only the task field with this:

```
Enum.map(conn.assigns.todos, fn(x)->x[:task] end)
```

We map the `todos` structure assigned to the connection and define an anonymous function to extract only the `task` key. The function defined in the view is `todos/1`. In step 2, we use the result of the function in a list comprehension:

```
<%= for t <- todos @conn do %>
  <li><%= t %></li>
<% end %>
```

The file extension is for the markup file is `html.eex`, which means that we are using HTML with embedded Elixir code for our template. The preceding block defining the list comprehension mixes HTML and Elixir. Elixir code is declared inside `<% %>`, and when we append the = sign, it means that the expression "appears" in the result.

> The code to render the `todos` list of maps mixes HTML and Elixir, as shown here:
> ```
> # start of block. Each entry in todos that will be
> represented by t
> <%= for t <- todos @conn do %>
> # output the value of t inside an html li tag
> <li><%= t %></li>
> #close the block
> <% end %>
> ```

There's more...

In our case, we only assign the `todos` data, but if we need to pass multiple values into the view, it's just a matter of calling `assign` several times in the controller and connecting these calls with the pipe operator (| >). The `assign` call returns the connection (`conn`), and it would be passed as the first value for subsequent `assign` function calls.

As a quick example, we will pass the `todos` and two messages to the view by writing the following code:

```
defmodule Todo.TodosController do
  use Phoenix.Controller

  plug :action
  plug :render

  def index(conn, _params) do
    todos = [%{id: 1, task: "Write the other controller actions!",
created_at: "2014-12-13", status: "pending"}, %{id: 2, task: "Create
Views", created_at: "2014-12-13", status: "pending"}]
    conn
    |> assign(:todos, todos)
    |> assign(:message_one, "Hello")
    |> assign(:message_two, "World!")
  end
end
```

Implementing topics

Topics in Phoenix are a form of implementing the publisher-subscriber pattern.

In this recipe, we will create a simple counter in a form of a function that will subscribe a channel.

In `TodosController`, we will broadcast an event every time a request is made to the index action. The counter will then receive the notification and will output a message to the console with the number of times the action was called.

Getting ready

To get started, we will take the code resulting from the previous recipe. Open a code editor and prepare to add pub/sub to the Phoenix application.

How to do it...

To implement topics in the Phoenix application, follow these steps:

1. Edit `TodoController` to make it look like this:

   ```
   defmodule Todo.TodosController do
   ```

```
use Phoenix.Controller

plug :action
plug :render

def index(conn, _params) do
  todos = [%{id: 1, task: "Write the other controller actions!",
created_at: "2014-12-13", status: "pending"}, %{id: 2, task:
"Create Views", created_at: "2014-12-13", status: "pending"}]

  # BROADCAST
  Phoenix.PubSub.broadcast "counter_channel", { :action,
controller: "Todos", action: "index" }

  assign(conn, :todos, todos)
end
end
```

2. Create a new `lib/todo/access_counter.ex` file and add the following code:

```
defmodule Todo.AccessCounter do
  def start_link do
    counter = 0
    sub = spawn_link(Todo.AccessCounter, :count, [counter])
    Phoenix.PubSub.subscribe(sub, "counter_channel")
    {:ok, sub}
  end
  def count(counter) do
    receive do
      { :action, params } ->
        counter = counter + 1
        IO.puts "Action #{params[:action]} in controller
#{params[:controller]} called #{counter} times!"

      _ ->
    end
    count(counter)
  end
end
```

3. Register the new file as a worker under the supervision tree of the application. In the `lib/todo.ex` file, define children this way:

```
children = [
  worker(Todo.AccessCounter, [])
]
```

4. Start the application (`mix phoenix.start`) and visit `http://localhost:4000/todos`. Refresh the page several times and the console will display something similar to this:

```
20:44:18.652 request_id=SGu5Bs7IHfnS/oxHbPlY [info] GET /todos
20:44:18.779 request_id=SGu5Bs7IHfnS/oxHbPlY [debug] Processing by
Todo.TodosController.index/2
  Parameters: %{"format" => "html"}
  Pipelines: [:browser]
Action index in controller Todos called 5 times!
```

How it works...

In step 1, when we add `Phoenix.PubSub.broadcast "counter_channel", { :action, controller: "Todos", action: "index" }` to the controller action, we are notifying "everyone" listening to the `counter_channel` channel. This means that every **subscriber** of the channel will become aware of the message being **published**.

In step 2, we define a module that subscribes to `counter_channel`. Generically, the module spawns a process that subscribes `counter_channel`, executing the `count/1` function every time a message arrives in the subscribed channel. The subscription is performed with this code:

```
Phoenix.PubSub.subscribe(sub, "counter_channel")
```

To have the module defined in step 2 running, we need to register it in the application's supervision tree. We do that in step 3 by registering the `Todo.AccessCounter` module as a worker.

Protecting the Phoenix app with SSL

In a production scenario, it will be likely for a Phoenix application to listen to requests using a secure protocol. HTTPS will be used in detriment of plain HTTP.

To accept connections securely, we need to launch the application with SSL support.

Fortunately, in Phoenix, configuring SSL is quite simple.

Getting ready

In a Phoenix application, place the `*.key` and `*.cert` files under the `priv` directory.

How to do it...

To configure SSL in a Phoenix application, we will need to add the following to the `config/prod.exs` file:

```
config :phoenix, Todo.Router,
  https: [port: 443,
          host: "example.com",
          keyfile: System.get_env("YOUR_SSL_KEY_FILE"),
          certfile: System.get_env("YOUR_APP_SSL_CERT_FILE")],
```

How it works...

We insert the configuration for HTTPS connections by defining the values of the port where the application will listen (443 is the default HTTPS port), the name of the host (the host for which the certificate files were generated), and the location of the certificate files.

As this is an OTP application, these files will be searched under the `priv` directory on the application's root.

By inserting the configuration code in the `prod.exs` file under the `conf` directory of the application, we are only enabling SSL for the production environment. This way, our application will run by listening on HTTP in the development and test environments.

8
Interactions

This chapter will cover the following recipes:

- ▶ Using Redis and Postgres
- ▶ Using OS commands from within Elixir
- ▶ Getting Twitter data

Introduction

In this chapter, we will perform some tasks, such as querying social media websites, interacting with the underlying operating system, implementing pub-sub, and connecting our Elixir applications to any other system using Redis. These recipes will be a little longer, given that the tasks are a little more elaborate or extended than those in the recipes from the previous chapters.

Using Redis and Postgres

In this recipe, we will be using Redis and Postgres. The idea is to exemplify how we can interact with these applications. Redis will be used as a message broker. We will implement the pub-sub pattern. Using the Redis console, we will **publish** messages on a specific channel, and our Elixir application will be **subscribed** to that channel and will retrieve those messages, saving them in a relational database (Postgres) afterwards.

The idea behind the use of Redis is to show you how we can use it to pass messages between applications. If we have two Erlang or Elixir applications, we can connect them and pass messages between them without using any message broker. It is even recommended that you not use any intermediate non-Elixir or non-Erlang application, because we would then have to add the overhead of data marshaling and unmarshaling. Between applications running in the Erlang VM, however, marshaling and unmarshaling are not required. However, what if we want to connect two or more applications developed in Elixir and Ruby, for instance?

This is where Redis comes in handy. More robust and elaborate applications exist—RabbitMQ, for instance—but for the purposes of this recipe, and for most simple message passing needs via pub/sub, Redis is fast, simple, and really easy to use.

As for the use of Postgres, we could definitely choose ETS, DETS, or Mnesia. These are solutions that come for free in Elixir. They are included in the Erlang runtime.

However, as the idea of this chapter is to show you how to interact, Postgres seems to be a good candidate, being one of the most robust RDBMS that are used.

After this longer than usual introduction, let's get started with building an application that will listen for messages, and as soon as they arrive, it will store them in a database.

Getting ready

In this recipe, we will need to have Redis and Postgres installed. Please refer to *Appendix, Installation and Further Reading,* for detailed instructions on how to install both applications.

After making sure both applications are installed, we need to create a database that can be used with our application. We will name it `elixir_cookbook`. To do this, open a terminal window and insert this command:

```
> createdb elixir_cookbook
```

How to do it...

To create our application, we will follow these steps:

1. Create a new application:

   ```
   > mix new redis_and_postgresql --sup
   ```

2. Add the dependencies to `mix.exs`:

   ```
   defp deps do
     [
        { :exredis, github: "artemeff/exredis", tag: "0.1.0" },
        { :postgrex, "~> 0.7.0" },
        { :ecto, "~> 0.7.1" }
     ]
   end
   ```

3. Add `postgrex` and `ecto` to the `applications` list to be started with the application:

   ```
   def application do
     [applications: [:logger, :postgrex, :ecto],
   ```

```
    mod: {RedisAndPostgresql, []}]
  end
```

4. Fetch the dependencies and compile them:

```
> mix deps.get && mix deps.compile
```

5. Create the `redis` and `postgres` folders under the `lib` directory.

6. Create the `lib/redis/subscriber.ex` module with the following content:

```
defmodule Redis.Subscriber do
  use GenServer
  use Exredis
  require Record
  Record.defrecord :state, [client: nil, client_sub: nil]

  @server               __MODULE__
  @redis_url            "127.0.0.1"
  @redis_port           "6379"
  @notification_channel "elixir_cookbook"
  @name                 :pubsub

  def start_link do
    :gen_server.start_link({:local, @server}, __MODULE__, [], [])
  end

  def init(_options\\[]) do
    client_sub = Exredis.Sub.start
    client = Exredis.start_using_connection_string("redis://#{@
redis_url}:#{@redis_port}")
    :global.register_name(@name, client)
    _pid = Kernel.self
    state = state(client: client, client_sub: client_sub)
    # Register the subscriber function
    client_sub |> Exredis.Sub.subscribe @notification_channel,
fn(msg) -> Redis.MsgPusher.send(msg) end
    {:ok, state}
  end

  def terminate(_reason, state) do
    # close redis connection
    client_sub = :erlang.list_to_pid(state.client_sub)
    client_sub |> Exredis.Sub.stop
    client = :erlang.list_to_pid(state.client)
```

```
      client |> Exredis.stop
      :ok
    end

  end
```

7. Create the `lib/redis/msg_pusher.ex` module and add this code to it:

```elixir
defmodule Redis.MsgPusher do

  def send(msg) do
    case msg do
      {:message, _, extracted_msg, _} ->
        IO.puts "#{log_time} [REDIS Msg Received] #{inspect msg}"
        Postgres.Db.save_message(extracted_msg)

      _ ->
    end
  end

  defp log_time do
    {{year, month, day}, {hour, minute, second}} = :erlang.now |>
  :calendar.now_to_local_time
    "[#{year}/#{month}/#{day} #{hour}:#{minute}:#{second}]"
  end

end
```

8. Add `Redis.Subscriber` to the application supervision tree in the `redis_and_postgresql.ex` file:

```elixir
children = [
    worker(Redis.Subscriber, [])
  ]
```

9. Create the `lib/postgres/repo.ex` module and edit it so that it looks like this:

```elixir
defmodule Postgres.Repo do
  use Ecto.Repo, adapter: Ecto.Adapters.Postgres

  def conf do
    # ecto://<USER>:<PASSWORD>@<HOST>/<DATABASE>
    parse_url "ecto://username@localhost/elixir_cookbook"
  end

  # define the place where to store migrations !
```

```
    def priv do
      app_dir(:redis_and_postgresql, "priv/repo")
    end
  end
```

10. Create the `lib/postgres/message.ex` module and add these lines:

```
defmodule Postgres.Message do
  use Ecto.Model

  schema "messages" do
    field :message_from,      :string
    field :message_to,        :string
    field :message_text,      :string
  end

end
```

11. Generate a migration:

```
> mix ecto.gen.migration Repo create_messages
```

12. Add some SQL to the migration to define the table for the `Message` model. The file is `priv/repo/migrations/<timestamp>_create_messages.exs`:

```
defmodule Repo.Migrations.CreateMessages do
  use Ecto.Migration

  def up do
    "CREATE TABLE IF NOT EXISTS messages(id serial primary key,
message_from text, message_to text, message_text text)"
  end

  def down do
    "DROP TABLE messages"
  end
end
```

13. Run the migration to prepare the database:

```
> mix ecto.migrate Repo
```

 To revert all migrations, the command is as follows:

```
mix ecto.rollback Repo --all
```

14. Create the `lib/postgres/db.ex` module and add this code to it:

```
defmodule Postgres.Db do
  import Ecto.Query, only: [from: 2]

  # alias to allow use of the struct
  # module that defines schema is Postgres.Message and not just
Message
  alias Postgres.Message

  # message will arrive as a string
  def save_message(message) when is_binary message do
    # message must be converted to a map
    [message_from, message_to, message_text] = String.
split(message, ",")
    msg = %Message{message_from: message_from, message_to:
message_to, message_text: message_text}
    Postgres.Repo.insert(msg)
  end

  def messages_from(from) do
    query = from m in Message, where: m.message_from == ^from
    Postgres.Repo.all(query)
  end

  def messages_to(to) do
    query = from m in Message, where: m.message_to == ^to
    Postgres.Repo.all(query)
  end

end
```

15. Add the `Postgres.Repo` module to the application's supervision tree:

```
children = [
    worker(Redis.Subscriber, []),
    worker(Postgres.Repo, [])
  ]
```

16. Start the application:

```
> iex -S mix
```

17. Open a Redis command-line session on another terminal:

```
> redis-cli
```

18. Start publishing messages on the channel and take a look at the application log:

```
127.0.0.1:6379> PUBLISH elixir_cookbook "foo,bar,hello"
127.0.0.1:6379> PUBLISH elixir_cookbook "foo,baz,hello"
127.0.0.1:6379> PUBLISH elixir_cookbook "bar,foo,hello"
127.0.0.1:6379> PUBLISH elixir_cookbook "baz,foo,hello"
```

The next screenshot shows you the messages being published on the channel:

```
Interactive Elixir (1.0.2) — press Ctrl+C to exit (type h() ENTER for help)
iex(1)> [2014/12/18 11:17:57] [REDIS Msg Received] {:message, "elixir_cookbook", "foo,bar,hello", #PID<0.126.0>}

11:17:57.505 [debug] INSERT INTO "messages" ("message_from", "message_text", "message_to") VALUES ($1, $2, $3) RETURNING "id" (24784µs)
[2014/12/18 11:19:10] [REDIS Msg Received] {:message, "elixir_cookbook", "foo,baz,hello", #PID<0.126.0>}

11:19:10.187 [debug] INSERT INTO "messages" ("message_from", "message_text", "message_to") VALUES ($1, $2, $3) RETURNING "id" (1430µs)
[2014/12/18 11:19:18] [REDIS Msg Received] {:message, "elixir_cookbook", "bar,foo,hello", #PID<0.126.0>}

11:19:18.725 [debug] INSERT INTO "messages" ("message_from", "message_text", "message_to") VALUES ($1, $2, $3) RETURNING "id" (1354µs)
[2014/12/18 11:19:29] [REDIS Msg Received] {:message, "elixir_cookbook", "baz,foo,hello", #PID<0.126.0>}

11:19:29.964 [debug] INSERT INTO "messages" ("message_from", "message_text", "message_to") VALUES ($1, $2, $3) RETURNING "id" (1296µs)
```

19. Now, it's time to take a look at our database. Let's retrieve some messages with these commands:

```
iex(2)> Postgres.Db.messages_from("foo")
iex(3)> Postgres.Db.messages_from("bar")
iex(4)> Postgres.Db.messages_to("baz")
iex(5)> Postgres.Db.messages_to("foo")
```

Here is the result of our queries:

```
iex(2)> Postgres.Db.messages_from("foo")

11:23:55.566 [debug] SELECT m0."id", m0."message_from", m0."message_to", m0."message_text" FROM "messages" AS m0 WHERE (m0."message_from" = $1::
text) (2440µs)
[%Postgres.Message{id: 64, message_from: "foo", message_text: "hello",
  message_to: "bar"},
 %Postgres.Message{id: 65, message_from: "foo", message_text: "hello",
  message_to: "baz"}]
iex(3)> Postgres.Db.messages_from("bar")

11:24:07.038 [debug] SELECT m0."id", m0."message_from", m0."message_to", m0."message_text" FROM "messages" AS m0 WHERE (m0."message_from" = $1::
text) (1294µs)
[%Postgres.Message{id: 66, message_from: "bar", message_text: "hello",
  message_to: "foo"}]
iex(4)> Postgres.Db.messages_to("baz")

11:24:15.182 [debug] SELECT m0."id", m0."message_from", m0."message_to", m0."message_text" FROM "messages" AS m0 WHERE (m0."message_to" = $1::te
xt) (1225µs)
[%Postgres.Message{id: 65, message_from: "foo", message_text: "hello",
  message_to: "baz"}]
iex(5)> Postgres.Db.messages_to("foo")

11:24:19.019 [debug] SELECT m0."id", m0."message_from", m0."message_to", m0."message_text" FROM "messages" AS m0 WHERE (m0."message_to" = $1::te
xt) (1183µs)
[%Postgres.Message{id: 66, message_from: "bar", message_text: "hello",
  message_to: "foo"},
 %Postgres.Message{id: 67, message_from: "baz", message_text: "hello",
  message_to: "foo"}]
iex(6)>
```

How it works...

In steps 1 to 4, we create the application and add the dependencies: `exredis` for Redis access, `postgrex` to interact with the database, and `ecto`, which is a DSL to write queries and interact with databases.

In step 5, we create two folders so that we can namespace our modules, making it easier to organize our code.

The module we define in step 6 is a GenServer and is responsible for establishing a connection to a Redis server. We see several annotations (`@server`, `@name`, `@redis_url`, `@notification_channel` and `@name`) that make it easier to change any of these values. We covered the use of annotations in the *Using module attributes as constants* recipe in *Chapter 4, Modules and Functions*.

In the `init` function, we initialize the process that will listen to the subscribed channel:

```
client_sub = Exredis.Sub.start
```

Start the connection to the Redis server:

```
client = Exredis.start_using_connection_string
    ("redis://#{@redis_url}:#{@redis_port}")
```

Register the name of this GenServer globally to make it accessible by name (`pubsub`):

```
:global.register_name(@name, client)
```

 Using the global registration allows us to refer to this process by its name from any node of a cluster.

Initialize the state of the GenServer where we basically store the PIDs of the processes that connect to Redis and the Redis channel:

```
state = state(client: client, client_sub: client_sub)
```

Finally, we determine the function to be invoked any time a new message arrives in the channel:

```
client_sub |> Exredis.Sub.subscribe "#{@notification_channel}",
fn(msg) -> Redis.MsgPusher.send(msg) end
```

The function is `send/1` and is defined in the `Redis.MsgPusher` module we defined in step 7. We use pattern matching to extract the message we get from Redis and then send `extracted_message` (the actual message) to the function that will save the message in the database (`Postgres.Db.save_message`):

```
{:message, _, extracted_msg, _} ->
```

```
       IO.puts "#{log_time} [REDIS Msg Received] #{inspect msg}"
       Postgres.Db.save_message(extracted_msg)
function
```

In step 8, we register the module responsible for the connection to Redis under the supervision tree. We don't want any glitches to deprive us from the connection to Redis!

Next, we start dealing with database-related logic. Our interaction with Postgres is achieved via Ecto.

In step 9, we begin by defining a repository. The `conf` function is responsible for determining the URL we use to connect to the database, and the `priv` function receives the name of the application and the location where the migrations will be stored as arguments.

In step 10, we define the schema for our messages. We determine the field names and their types.

In steps 11 and 12, we use a custom Ecto Mix task to generate a migration file, and we add SQL code to the migration. We define the database table that will hold our messages.

In step 13, we run the migration, and this effectively creates the database table.

Afterwards, we create the module that will interact with the database, which is `Postgres.Db`. The function we registered as the one to be triggered when the Redis client receives a message on the listening channel is defined in this module:

```
# message will arrive as a string
  def save_message(message) when is_binary message do
    # message must be converted to a map
    [message_from, message_to, message_text] =
      String.split(message, ",")
    msg = %Message{message_from: message_from, message_to:
      message_to, message_text: message_text}
    Postgres.Repo.insert(msg)
  end
```

We begin by splitting the string we receive (comma-separated) and pattern match it to get the `message_from`, `message_to`, and `message_text` fields that we will use to create a map that we insert into the database via the `Postgres.Repo` module.

 By creating a schema in the `Postgres.Message` module, Ecto defines a struct with the fields declared in that schema.

We also need to add the `Postgresql.DB` module to the application's supervision tree similar to what we did with `Redis.Subscriber`.

In the following steps, we use the Redis command line to publish messages on the `elixir_cookbook` channel and watch them being logged in our application's console.

In the last step, we perform some queries to retrieve the data stored in the database.

These queries are defined in the `Postgres.Db` module:

```
def messages_from(from) do
  query = from m in Message, where: m.message_from == ^from
  Postgres.Repo.all(query)
end

def messages_to(to) do
  query = from m in Message, where: m.message_to == ^to
  Postgres.Repo.all(query)
end
```

We start by building a query, and then we execute it via our `Repo` module. The syntax for the queries is straightforward and is compared with LINQ by a few. The queries are also composable and type-safe!

You may have noticed the `^` operator before `from` and `to`. This operator is overloaded by Ecto, and it's used when we need to access values outside Ecto because Ecto queries are under their own syntax.

Using OS commands from within Elixir

It is possible to interact with the underlying operating system, execute OS commands, and get the result in our Elixir applications.

To do this, we will be using Alexei Sholik's **porcelain** (`https://hex.pm/packages/porcelain`).

We will build a very simple application that will accept a string defining a path and will return a list containing the entries for that path. We will use the `ls unix` command without leaving our Elixir application! We will also define a generic run function that will allow the running of any command we pass as the argument.

How to do it...

To create an application that interacts with the underlying operating system, we will follow these steps:

1. Create a new application:

```
> mix new os_commands
```

2. Add the porcelain app as a dependency in the `mix.exs` file:

```
defp deps do
  [{:porcelain, "~> 2.0"}]
end
```

3. Register porcelain into the list of applications (inside the `mix.exs` file):

```
def application do
  [applications: [:logger, :porcelain]]
end
```

4. Get the dependency and compile it:

```
> mix deps.get && mix deps.compile
```

5. Define the `list` function that will return the entries in a given directory by entering the following code in `lib/os_commands.ex`:

```
def list(path \\ ".") do
  %Result{out: output, status: status} = Porcelain.exec("ls
    #{path}")
  IO.puts output
End
```

First of all, we will include the following in our module:

```
alias Porcelain.Result
```

This will allow us to use the `Result` struct defined by porcelain in a more convenient way.

6. Define the `run` function that will run a command passed as the argument by entering the following code in `lib/os_commands.ex`:

```
def run(command, options \\"") do
  %Result{out: output, status: status} =
    Porcelain.shell(command, [args])
  IO.puts output
end
```

7. Compile and start the application:

```
> mix compile && iex -S mix
```

8. Lastly, let's try to inspect some of our directories:

```
iex(1)> OsCommands.list
README.md
_build
config
```

```
        deps
        lib
        mix.exs
        mix.lock
        test
        :ok

        iex(2)> OsCommands.list "/usr"
        X11
        X11R6
        bin
        include
        lib
        libexec
        local
        sbin
        share
        standalone
        :ok
```

9. Now, let's run some commands:

```
        iex(3)> OsCommands.run("date")
        Mon Dec 8 20:15:25 WET 2014
        :ok
```

10. We can even see the content of modules:

```
        iex(4)> OsCommands.run("cat", "lib/os_commands.ex")
        defmodule OsCommands do
          alias Porcelain.Result

          def list(path \\ ".") do
            %Result{out: output, status: status} = Porcelain.exec("ls",
        [path])
            IO.puts output
          end

          def run(command, options \\"") do
```

```
    %Result{out: output, status: status} = Porcelain.
shell("#{command} #{options}")

    IO.puts output
  end
end


  :ok
```

How it works...

After creating the application and adding porcelain as a dependency, we have to configure it to run automatically. In step 3, we add porcelain to the list of applications that will be bootstrapped once the `OsCommands` application starts.

In steps 5 and 6, we define two functions. The first one, `list`, performs an `ls` command, and if no option for the path is passed, it defaults to the `application` directory. The `run` function is more generic and allows you to execute any command available in the OS.

There's more...

It is possible to define the input as a file or a stream and the same goes for output as well. Porcelain is a very powerful tool that allows us to build things such as filesystem monitors that perform actions any time a file is changed. The most impressive thing is that it allows us to leverage the power of the underlying operating system, expanding the available options we have in Elixir.

See also

▶ It is possible to use the Goon driver with porcelain. Goon is developed in Go and allows access to more features with porcelain, specifically, the ability to signal EOF to the external program and also send an OS signal to the program.

▶ For more information on porcelain, refer to the documentation available at `http://porcelain.readthedocs.org/`.

Getting Twitter data

In this recipe, we will build an application that will query the Twitter timeline for a given word and will display any new tweet with that keyword in real time. We will be using an Elixir twitter client **extwitter** as well as an Erlang application to deal with OAuth. We will wrap all in a phoenix web application.

Getting ready

Before getting started, we need to register a new application with Twitter to get the API keys that will allow the authentication and use of Twitter's API. To do this, we will go to `https://apps.twitter.com` and click on the **Create New App** button. After following the steps, we will have access to four items that we need: `consumer_key`, `consumer_secret`, `access_token`, and `access_token_secret`.

These values can be used directly in the application or setup as environment variables in an initialization file for bash or zsh (if using Unix).

After getting the keys, we are ready to start building the application.

How to do it...

To begin with building the application, we need to follow these steps:

1. Create a new Phoenix application:

   ```
   > mix phoenix.new phoenix_twitter_stream code/phoenix_twitter_
   stream
   ```

    For more information on how to create a Phoenix application, please refer to the *Creating a Phoenix application* recipe in *Chapter 7, Cowboy and Phoenix*.

2. Add the dependencies in the `mix.exs` file:

   ```
   defp deps do
     [
       {:phoenix, "~> 0.8.0"},
       {:cowboy, "~> 1.0"},
       {:oauth, github: "tim/erlang-oauth"},
       {:extwitter, "~> 0.1"}
     ]
   end
   ```

3. Get the dependencies and compile them:

   ```
   > mix deps.get && mix deps.compile
   ```

4. Configure the application to use the Twitter API keys by adding the configuration block with the keys we got from Twitter in the *Getting ready* section. Edit `lib/phoenix_twitter_stream.ex` so that it looks like this:

   ```
   defmodule PhoenixTweeterStream do
   ```

```
  use Application

  def start(_type, _args) do
    import Supervisor.Spec, warn: false

    ExTwitter.configure(
      consumer_key: System.get_env("SMM_TWITTER_CONSUMER_KEY"),
      consumer_secret: System.get_env("SMM_TWITTER_CONSUMER_
SECRET"),
      access_token: System.get_env("SMM_TWITTER_ACCESS_TOKEN"),
      access_token_secret: System.get_env("SMM_TWITTER_ACCESS_
TOKEN_SECRET")
    )

    children = [
      # Start the endpoint when the application starts
      worker(PhoenixTweeterStream.Endpoint, []),

      # Here you could define other workers and supervisors as
children
      # worker(PhoenixTweeterStream.Worker, [arg1, arg2, arg3]),
    ]

    opts = [strategy: :one_for_one, name: PhoenixTweeterStream.
Supervisor]
    Supervisor.start_link(children, opts)
  end

  def config_change(changed, _new, removed) do
    PhoenixTweeterStream.Endpoint.config_change(changed, removed)
    :ok
  end
end
```

In this case, the keys are stored as environment variables, so we use the `System.get_env` function:

```
System.get_env("SMM_TWITTER_CONSUMER_KEY") (...)
```

If you don't want to set the keys as environment variables, the keys can be directly declared as strings this way:

```
consumer_key: "this-is-an-example-key" (...)
```

5. Define a module that will handle the query for new tweets in the `lib/phoenix_twitter_stream/tweet_streamer.ex` file, and add the following code:

```
defmodule PhoenixTwitterStream.TweetStreamer do

  def start(socket, query) do
    stream = ExTwitter.stream_filter(track: query)
    for tweet <- stream do
      Phoenix.Channel.reply(socket, "tweet:stream", tweet)
    end
  end

end
```

6. Create the channel that will handle the tweets in the `web/channels/tweets.ex` file:

```
defmodule PhoenixTwitterStream.Channels.Tweets do
  use Phoenix.Channel
  alias PhoenixTwitterStream.TweetStreamer

  def join("tweets", %{"track" => query}, socket) do
    spawn(fn() -> TweetStreamer.start(socket, query) end)
    {:ok, socket}
  end

end
```

7. Edit the application router (`/web/router.ex`) to register the websocket handler and the `tweets` channel. The file will look like this:

```
defmodule PhoenixTwitterStream.Router do
  use Phoenix.Router

  pipeline :browser do
    plug :accepts, ~w(html)
    plug :fetch_session
    plug :fetch_flash
    plug :protect_from_forgery
  end

  pipeline :api do
    plug :accepts, ~w(json)
```

```
    end

    socket "/ws" do
      channel "tweets", PhoenixTwitterStream.Channels.Tweets
    end

    scope "/", PhoenixTwitterStream do
      pipe_through :browser # Use the default browser stack

      get "/", PageController, :index
    end
  end
```

8. Replace the index template (`web/templates/page/index.html.eex`) content with this:

```
<div class="row">
  <div class="col-lg-12">
    <ul id="tweets"></ul>
  </div>

  <script src="/js/phoenix.js" type="text/javascript"></script>
  <script src="https://code.jquery.com/jquery-2.1.1.js"
type="text/javascript"></script>
  <script type="text/javascript">
    var my_track = "programming";
    var socket = new Phoenix.Socket("ws://" + location.host + "/
ws");
    socket.join("tweets", {track: my_track}, function(chan){
      chan.on("tweet:stream", function(message){
        console.log(message);
        $('#tweets').prepend($('<li>').text(message.text));
        });
      });
    });
  </script>
</div>
```

9. Start the application:

```
> mix phoenix.server
```

10. Go to `http://localhost:4000/` and after a few seconds, tweets should start arriving and the page will be updated to display every new tweet at the top.

Get Started

- Poweredup Up with #SandraBeck and Linda Franklin on #ToginetRadio #Best #Web #Talk #Programming http://t.co/hsWfFkNi9a
- #Best #Web #Talk #Programming http://t.co/jBvMfYVDV2 Poweredup Up with #SandraBeck and Linda Franklin on #ToginetRadio
- #DamienMizdow is still the best part of @WWE programming! #wwe #WWETLC #TagTeamTitles
- RT @AdobeEdu: Try an #hourofcode with our free courses on programming. Earn a certificate of completion with @adobeknowhow http://t.co/TiVN...
- #Best #Web #Talk #Programming http://t.co/MNJxHQE9v0 Poweredup Up with #SandraBeck and Linda Franklin on #ToginetRadio
- The only downside to watching 1 star Netflix programming is it usually gets cancelled after 1 season & now I'll never know what happened!
- RT @programming_j: UIデザインで使いたいアプリケーション(止まっている状態のUI制作関連編) #2014.09版 - たぶん、ねむたくなる http://t.co/4qT6JQo4Yr #programming
- RT @AdobeEdu: Try an #hourofcode with our free courses on programming. Earn a certificate of completion with @adobeknowhow http://t.co/TiVN...
- #Best #Web #Talk #Programming http://t.co/GG1qtdekuZ Powered Up Talk Radio with @SandraBeck and Linda Franklin on @ToginetRadio
- I really want to hard code in #WebGL. Not wanting to code utilizing third party libraries. Where is the hard work, in that? #programming
- @yancyvance Bash programming should be standard topic in Operating Systems classes. As Assistant Dean, I order a content review immediately
- @Toni_Pipicelli @shaunheron #TheLuckyCountry Off'l Vid: http://t.co/BZ3SsRinIl New fr @the3basics. Pls add to on-air programming #Wallnuts
- @lafergs In what world should those things ever combine? And also, have you taken control of WWE programming?

How it works...

We start by creating a Phoenix application. We could have created a simple application to output the tweets in the console or even used something like what was implemented in the *Implementing a websocket handler* recipe in *Chapter 7, Cowboy and Phoenix*. However, Phoenix is a great choice for our purposes, displaying a web page with tweets getting updated in real time via websockets!

In step 2, we add the dependencies needed to work with the Twitter API. We use parroty's extwitter Elixir application (`https://hex.pm/packages/extwitter`) and Tim's erlang-oauth application (`https://github.com/tim/erlang-oauth/`). After getting the dependencies and compiling them, we add the Twitter API keys to our application (step 4). These keys will be used to authenticate against Twitter where we previously registered our application.

In step 5, we define a function that, when started, will query Twitter for any tweets containing a specific query.

The `stream = ExTwitter.stream_filter(track: query)` line defines a stream that is returned by the `ExTwitter` application and is the result of filtering Twitter's timeline, extracting only the entries (tracks) that contain the defined query.

The next line, which is `for tweet <- stream do Phoenix.Channel.reply(socket, "tweet:stream", tweet)`, is a stream comprehension. For every new entry in the stream defined previously, send the entry through a Phoenix channel.

Step 6 is where we define the channel. This channel is like a websocket handler. Actually, we define a `join` function:

```
def join(socket, "stream", %{"track" => query}) do
  reply socket, "join", %{status: "connected"}
  spawn(fn() -> TweetStreamer.start(socket, query) end)
  {:ok, socket}
end
```

It is here, when the websocket connection is performed, that we initialize the module defined in step 5 in the spawn call. This function receives a query string defined in the frontend code as `track` and passes that string to `ExTwitter`, which will use it as the filter.

In step 7, we register and mount the websocket handler in the router using `use Phoenix.Router.Socket, mount: "/ws"`, and we define the channel and its handler module using `channel "tweets", PhoenixTwitterStream.Channels.Tweets`.

The channel definition must occur outside any scope definition!

If we tried to define it, say, right before `get "/", PageController, :index`, the compiler would issue an error message and the application wouldn't even start.

The last code we need to add is related to the frontend. In step 8, we mix HTML and JavaScript on the same file that will be responsible for displaying the root page and establishing the websocket connection with the server. We use a phoenix.js library helper (`<script src="/js/phoenix.js" type="text/javascript"></script>`), providing some functions to deal with Phoenix websockets and channels.

We will take a closer look at some of the code in the frontend:

```
// initializes the query … in this case filter the timeline for
// all tweets containing "programming"
var my_track = "programming";
// initialize the websocket connection. The endpoint is /ws.  //(we
already have registered with the phoenix router on step 7)
var socket = new Phoenix.Socket("ws://" + location.host + "/ws");
// in here we join the channel 'tweets'
```

```
// this code triggers the join function we saw on step 6
// when a new tweet arrives from the server via websocket
// connection it is prepended to the existing tweets in the page
socket.join("tweets", "stream", {track: my_track}, function(chan){
     chan.on("tweet:stream", function(message){
        $('#tweets').prepend($('<li>').text(message.text));
        });
     });
```

There's more...

If you wish to see the page getting updated really fast, select a more *popular* word for the query.

See also

▸ In *Chapter 7, Cowboy and Phoenix*, there are several recipes related to the Phoenix framework, from creating an application to setting up each of the components. If you wish, refer to these recipes to gain a better understanding of Phoenix.

Installation and Further Reading

Now that we have learnt about Elixir, it is a good idea to also see which useful websites are available that will help us to enhance our knowledge. In this appendix, we will cover how to install Elixir, PostgreSQL, and Redis, and we will look at a few external website links that will help us with further reading.

Let's start with the installation.

Installing Elixir

We need to visit `http://elixir-lang.org/install.html` for all the documentation needed to install Elixir.

This page will help you with all the information on installing Elixir and Erlang on major operating systems.

Installing PostgreSQL

Please visit the following links to install PostgreSQL:

- ▶ Information on several operating systems' installation process for PostgreSQL can be found at `https://wiki.postgresql.org/wiki/Detailed_installation_guides`
- ▶ PostgreSQL can be downloaded from `http://www.postgresql.org/download/`

Installing Redis

The following links will help you get up and running with Redis:

- Visit `http://redis.io` to get to the Redis homepage
- The download page and installation instructions can be accessed at `http://redis.io/download`
- If you want to go through the official documentation for Redis, visit `http://redis.io/documentation`

Some useful links

Further reading is always important to broaden your knowledge base. Let's go through some of the useful links that will help us gain more insight.

Elixir

Here are a few references on Elixir:

- The Elixir homepage is available at `http://elixir-lang.org`.
- The *Getting Started* guide is available at `http://elixir-lang.org/getting-started/introduction.html`.
- The Elixir documentation is available at `http://elixir-lang.org/docs.html`.
- Packages (the Elixir package manager) can be accessed at `https://hex.pm`.
- The source code can be accessed at `https://github.com/elixir-lang/elixir`.

The Phoenix framework

The homepage of the Phoenix framework can be accessed at `http://www.phoenixframework.org`.

Erlang

The Erlang homepage is available at `http://www.erlang.org`.

The official documentation for Erlang can accessed at `http://www.erlang.org/doc.html`.

Index

immutability of data
  about 39, 40
  demonstrating 40-42
init function 142 172
insert_replaced function 71
integers 44
Interactive Elixir. *See* IEx
is_binary function 107
is_list function 107

J

join function 209

K

key/value store
  about 128
  creating, with map 54-56
keyword list
  about 45
  creating 45-47
  manipulating 45-47

L

lazy (even infinite) sequences
  generating 58-62
List.foldl/3 function 41
lists
  adding, with ++ operator 42, 43
  subtracting, with – operator 42, 43
  tuples, combining into 44, 45
locate function 121

M

map
  about 54
  used, for creating key/value store 54, 55
Map.new/0 function 55
messages
  between processes, sending 110-113
metadata
  reading, from MP3 files 83-89
  references 89

writing, from MP3 files 83-88
Mix
  about 8
  used, for creating Elixir application 21-23
module attributes
  using, as constants 93, 94
module directives
  using 98-101
modules
  about 91
  compiling 9-11
  documenting 96-98
  loading 9-11
  namespacing 92, 93
  using, in scripted mode 101, 102
MP3 files
  metadata, reading 83-89
  metadata, writing 83-88
multiple concurrent computations
  performing, with Task module 117-122

N

named nodes
  creating 131-133
nodes
  connecting 133-135
Node.spawn function 136

O

Observer
  used, for inspecting system 19-21
  using, for inspecting processes 146-148
  using, for inspecting supervisors 146-148
Open Telecom Platform (OTP) 137
operations
  combining, with |> operator 74-77
OptionParse.parse function 81
OS commands
  using, from Elixir 200-203
OTP application
  packaging 152-156
  releasing 152-156

P

pattern matching
HTTPoison response 50-53
using 48, 49
using, in function definitions 104-107
patterns
string codepoints, replacing with 69-71
**Perl Compatible Regular Expressions
     (PCRE) 72**
Phoenix
about 160
framework, URL 212
Phoenix application
creating 173-176
protecting, with SSL 188-189
topics, implementing 186-188
phone_book.ex module
creating 125-127
porcelain
about 200-203
URL 200
Postgres
using 191-200
PostgreSQL
installing 211
URL 211
print_each_from_list function 107
print function 105, 106
process ID (PID) 112
Project Gutenberg
URL 81

R

range
used, for slicing strings 71, 72
read-eval-print-loop (REPL) 8
recursive function 105
Redis
installing 212
references 212
URL 212
using 191-199
Regex.compile! function 74

regular expressions
using 73, 74
resource
file, streaming as 62-64
REST
URL 179
routes
defining 176-180
run/1 function 37
running system
updating 156, 157

S

scripted mode
module, using 101, 102
search_user function 141
sequential function 121, 122
spawn_link function 112
SSL
used, for protecting Phoenix application 189
start_link function 145
stateful server process
creating 122-125
static files
serving 163-168
string codepoints
replacing, with patterns 69-71
strings
joining 66, 67
slicing, with range 71, 72
splitting 67-69
String.slice/2 function 72
String.split_at function 69
sum function 104
supervised application
generating 28, 29
supervisor
creating 143-145
implementing 145
URL 145
symbol 17
system
inspecting, in IEx 17, 18
inspecting, with Observer 19-21
System.get_env function 205

Thank you for buying
Elixir Cookbook

About Packt Publishing

Packt, pronounced 'packed', published its first book, *Mastering phpMyAdmin for Effective MySQL Management*, in April 2004, and subsequently continued to specialize in publishing highly focused books on specific technologies and solutions.

Our books and publications share the experiences of your fellow IT professionals in adapting and customizing today's systems, applications, and frameworks. Our solution-based books give you the knowledge and power to customize the software and technologies you're using to get the job done. Packt books are more specific and less general than the IT books you have seen in the past. Our unique business model allows us to bring you more focused information, giving you more of what you need to know, and less of what you don't.

Packt is a modern yet unique publishing company that focuses on producing quality, cutting-edge books for communities of developers, administrators, and newbies alike. For more information, please visit our website at www.packtpub.com.

About Packt Open Source

In 2010, Packt launched two new brands, Packt Open Source and Packt Enterprise, in order to continue its focus on specialization. This book is part of the Packt open source brand, home to books published on software built around open source licenses, and offering information to anybody from advanced developers to budding web designers. The Open Source brand also runs Packt's open source Royalty Scheme, by which Packt gives a royalty to each open source project about whose software a book is sold.

Writing for Packt

We welcome all inquiries from people who are interested in authoring. Book proposals should be sent to author@packtpub.com. If your book idea is still at an early stage and you would like to discuss it first before writing a formal book proposal, then please contact us; one of our commissioning editors will get in touch with you.

We're not just looking for published authors; if you have strong technical skills but no writing experience, our experienced editors can help you develop a writing career, or simply get some additional reward for your expertise.

PACKT PUBLISHING

open source
community experience distilled

Ruby and MongoDB Web Development Beginner's Guide

ISBN: 978-1-84951-502-3   Paperback: 332 pages

Create dynamic web applications by combining the power of Ruby and MongoDB

1. Step-by-step instructions and practical examples to creating web applications with Ruby and MongoDB.

2. Learn to design the object model in a NoSQL way.

3. Create objects in Ruby and map them to MongoDB.

Instant RubyMine Assimilation

ISBN: 978-1-84969-876-4   Paperback: 66 pages

Utilize the RubyMine IDE to develop your own Ruby on Rails applications

1. Learn something new in an Instant! A short, fast, focused guide delivering immediate results.

2. Incorporate features of RubyMine into your everyday Ruby and Ruby on Rails development workflow.

3. Learn about the integrated testing and debugging tools to make your coding bulletproof and productive.

Please check **www.PacktPub.com** for information on our titles

Instant RubyMotion App Development

ISBN: 978-1-84969-652-4   Paperback: 54 pages

A jump start to quickly learn how to program iOS applications with the elegance and simplicity of Ruby

1. Learn something new in an Instant! A short, fast, focused guide delivering immediate results.

2. Learn the structure of iPhone and iPad applications.

3. Discover how to simplify iOS apps with Ruby.

RubyMotion iOS Development Essentials

ISBN: 978-1-84969-522-0   Paperback: 262 pages

Create apps that utilize iOS device capabilities without learning Objective-C

1. Get your iOS apps ready faster with RubyMotion.

2. Use iOS device capabilities such as GPS, camera, multitouch, and many more in your apps.

3. Learn how to test your apps and launch them on the AppStore.

4. Use Xcode with RubyMotion and extend your RubyMotion apps with Gems.

Please check **www.PacktPub.com** for information on our titles

www.ingramcontent.com/pod-product-compliance
Lightning Source LLC
Chambersburg PA
CBHW060548060326
40690CB00017B/3637